Top Entrepreneurs
and Their Businesses

Top Entrepreneurs
and Their Businesses

Robert B. Pile

illustrated with photographs

The Oliver Press, Inc.
Minneapolis

Library of Congress Cataloging-in-Publication Data

Pile, Robert B., 1918-
Top entrepreneurs and their businesses / Robert B. Pile.
p.   cm. — (Profiles)
Includes bibliographical references and index.
    Summary: Examines the lives of eight men and one woman, including Sam Walton, L.L. Bean, Walt Disney, and Rose Totino, who built once-small businesses into well-known enterprises.
ISBN 1-881508-04-8 : $14.95
1. Businessmen—United States—Biography—Juvenile literature.
2. Entrepreneurship—United States—Juvenile literature.
[1. Businessmen.]   I. Title. II. Series: Profiles (Minneapolis, Minn.)
HC102.5.A2P55 1993
338' .04' 092273—dc20
[B]

92-38267
CIP
AC

ISBN 1-881508-04-8
Profiles VI
Printed in the United States of America

99 98 97 96 95   8 7 6 5 4 3 2

Contents

Introduction

*T*his book is about success. Each chapter tells the story of how a man or woman started and built a successful business. The people in this book are neither star athletes, nor TV celebrities, nor musicians, nor astronauts. No, they are business people.

You may feel that business people cannot possibly be interesting. Nothing could be further from the truth! In fact, when you finish this book, I hope you will agree that the people you have read about in these pages have done exciting things, and have achieved—without exception—fascinating and even spectacular results.

Each person in this book had qualities that all successful individuals seem to have. You will meet these people and learn how these qualities contributed to the success of the companies they created.

The business leaders whose stories you will read

were, or are, remarkable human beings, so remarkable that you may feel that their abilities make them superior individuals. But if you think about their lives, you will realize that each one is a lot like you.

Each started with an idea or a goal. Then he or she took that idea and built it into a company that provided either products or services. A *product*, of course, is different from a *service*. An example of a product is a Louisville Slugger baseball bat. An example of a service is Northwest Airlines.

We usually call people who have good ideas "creative." And we often associate the word *creative* with the ability to draw or write music or poetry. Of the people in this book, only Walt Disney could actually draw pictures. So, most of these people were not creative as we might normally think of the word.

If you look up the word in a dictionary, however, you will find that the definition does not mention drawing or writing or composing music. Your dictionary tells you that *creativity* is the ability to produce something original rather than imitating. True creativity is the ability to solve problems. In this book, you will see how the creativity of a few people helped to solve problems that no one before them could. In solving these problems, each person overcame the obstacles that confronted them.

Their ability to conquer obstacles may be what makes these people special. Their talent does not make them special. But if not talent, then what?

Determination to use that talent—to allow it to over-come obstacles—to solve problems—that is what makes these people different and successful. Yes, determination makes these people special.

An outstanding quality of business leaders is their courage to take risks. The people profiled here took risks at the beginning of their success stories and con-tinued to take risks throughout their careers. Every step of the way, they made risky business decisions, some so big that one mistake could have cost them their dream and could have put many employees out of work.

Business people who takes risks are often called by the French word *entrepreneurs*. In a free economy, entrepreneurs are very important. Without people who risk their money and time and reputation to start businesses, our country would not be what it is. The creation of jobs through the hard work of entrepre-neurs is vital to maintaining our way of life.

So, this book will give you a look at successful people—people who started and built famous compa-nies. Perhaps this book will inspire you to business success also. For success is not a matter of having exceptional talent, but rather of using whatever talent you have. When you use that talent and combine it with the determination to try and try and try again, your idea has a chance to succeed. Your chance for success, like the success of the people in this book, is in your own hands.

Less than three decades after the Wright brothers' first flight, Lewis Brittin built the foundation for one of the largest companies in aviation history—Northwest Airlines.

1

Lewis Brittin:
The Connecticut Colonel
and His Flying Dream

*T*o understand this story better, do some imagining. Forget who you are and put yourself back in time to the year 1926. You are very tall, and you look much like a college professor with your high, starched collar, wire-rimmed glasses, and stiff back. You are a veteran of the Spanish-American War, where you received your rank of lieutenant colonel. You are intensely interested in aviation, but you are not a pilot and, in fact, have never even flown in a plane. Your name is Lewis H. Brittin, and everyone calls you "Colonel."

You were born in Connecticut, and your childhood was full of hardship. An orphan, you went to boarding school where life was difficult. You loved the outdoors, and as a young man, you wandered around the hills of your state. You were a good athlete, and later you became captain of the Harvard baseball team, as well as a member of the rowing crew. You did not finish college, but joined the army, where you attained the rank you still carry. Until you were a young man, you were unsure whether to spell your name "Lewis" or "Louis."

With this as background, here is your story: Following World War I, business people and the general public expressed considerable interest in aviation. War stories about the heroics of army pilots filled the newspapers, and millions knew the names of the greatest "aces." The war had ended in 1918, and pilots were trying to find jobs in an otherwise expanding economy. However, despite the interest, aviation was not part of the thriving atmosphere. Nothing at that time was like the airline industry today. No United or American or Delta; no jumbo jets; no scheduled flights anywhere. The only truly organized flying was the postal service, and this had come about because trains, which were slow and unreliable, carried the mail. Sometimes a letter took a week, or even two, to go from New York to Chicago! The public demanded better service, and by 1920, U.S. Postal Service planes were flying one coast-to-coast route each day.

Connecting with this main route were dozens of feeder lines coming from every state. But because of many crashes and deaths, the public pressured the U.S. president, and Congress, to put airmail into the hands of private companies. One of the feeder lines at that time was operating out of the Twin Cities of St. Paul and Minneapolis, connecting to Chicago. But its first flight ended in a fatal crash and, within weeks, the line was in serious trouble.

The owner of the feeder line announced to the post office that his airline would go out of business on October 1, 1926. The first person to hear this news was Colonel Lewis Brittin. He was vice president and director of industrial development for the St. Paul Association—something like the chamber of commerce. His job was to promote St. Paul and the surrounding communities. The association put Brittin, then in his forties, in charge of all local business activities that would further this objective. He was a perfect choice.

In the founding of a company and its path to success, several people usually are involved. Thus, pointing to one individual and saying, "This is the person who made it go" is almost impossible. But Lewis Brittin *is* the man who set what is now Northwest Airlines on a direction that assured its development over the years.

Brittin had many talents: He had organizational skills and was very good at planning. He was, despite his formal appearance, an excellent salesman. He could win friends and inspire confidence, and when he established a goal, he was relentless in achieving it. Most of all, he had a quality that was priceless in the job he had to do—he had extraordinary vision; that is, he had an instinct for looking into the future and understanding what might happen 10, 20, and even 40 years into the future. He could grasp big ideas and see how they could come into play as time went by. Not all successful people have this gift, but Brittin did.

One of his first moves with the St. Paul Association was to get in touch with Henry Ford, the successful maker of automobiles in Detroit. Over a period of time, he persuaded Ford to build a car assembly plant on the Mississippi River between St. Paul and Minneapolis. Brittin had noticed an unused dam on the river, and his vision helped him to see that it could be used in manufacturing. (The St. Paul Ford plant still operates on that

Best known for making cars affordable to the average person, Henry Ford also contributed to the development of mass air travel.

site.) Brittin was neither rich nor the owner of any business. He was simply working for a paycheck on a civic enterprise, but his power was that he could act on his ideas. And his early meeting with Henry Ford was to be a key factor in the building of the airline.

Before October 1, 1926, when its owner announced that it would go out of business, Brittin visited various companies in an effort to convince them to take over the dying airline. He got nowhere, but he was not the kind to cave in simply because of an occasional defeat. He went back to Henry Ford. The two of them put together a group of Detroit business people who agreed to start Northwest Airways, Inc. They decided that the business would be owned in Michigan, but operated out of St. Paul.

They incorporated the new air company on September 1, 1926, just one month before the old contract was up. Brittin then went to Washington and persuaded post office officials to grant him a contract to fly the mail. (At this time, airlines did not fly passengers; they made their money, if any, flying the mail.)

In mid-September 1926, Brittin had no airplanes, no employees, no hangars, no office, and no telephone. All he had was a contract to get a brand-new airline started in a matter of days.

But another one of Brittin's talents was the courage to move decisively. Because he had no airplanes to start with, he rented two immediately, and he ordered three

:livered later. Flights began on October 1,
..e Twin Cities have had airmail service ever

..president of the airline was a man who lived in
Deu.. ,, but Colonel Brittin ran the business and often
against seemingly impossible obstacles. For example,
on the first flight with a passenger in 1927, the pilot had
to make a forced landing only 100 miles south of
Minneapolis. He called Brittin, who jumped into a
truck and drove down to pick up the mail, whereupon
the pilot got the plane fixed and took off from the field
in which he landed. And who actually sold the first passenger ticket? Why, Colonel Brittin, of course.

To help him manage the hundreds of daily details of
running an airline, Brittin brought from the St. Paul
Association a remarkable woman named Camille Stein.
Everyone called her "Rosie," because when asked how
things were, she always said "Everything's rosy." She
later became the first female officer of an airline and
was voted to the board of directors. An additional sign
of Brittin's sharp sense of values was that he placed a
woman in a job of great importance and helped her
grow along with the business. That seldom happened in
the 1920s. Among her many duties, "Rosie" Stein
trained stewardesses when airlines began carrying passengers.

In May 1927, the flying business got a huge boost
from the heroic flight across the Atlantic Ocean by
Charles A. Lindbergh. Lindbergh later became a consultant to Northwest and helped Brittin in many ways.

Camille "Rosie" Stein, seated in front of an air route map, worked closely with Lewis Brittin to establish Northwest Airlines.

With the airline now off and running, Brittin began to get more people from the Twin Cities involved in the business. As part of this project, he proved to be a shrewd publicity man and succeeded in getting many positive stories about Northwest into the newspapers. For example, when one of the new airplanes he had ordered had to land in a farmyard, he arranged to have a newspaper photographer there when the plane later took off. Curiously, the farm belonged to the pilot's mother and father, which resulted in more good stories. The colonel knew how to make the best of everything!

Through 1927 and 1928, Brittin sold more and more Northwest stock to people in the Twin Cities. Three of them then joined the board of directors. To prove that being rich was not necessary to becoming a part owner of an airline, Northwest's chief pilot, a young man named Charles "Speed" Holman, invested $2,000 to buy stock. Holman's salary at the time was just $4,000 a year!

In 1928, Brittin, with his eye on the future, wrote a long and thoughtful story about aviation and the airline business. He used this article to interest business investors and to get the U.S. government to think of flying as a serious and important new industry. Brittin also brought air service to smaller cities around Minnesota, including flights to the famous Mayo Clinic in Rochester. One of the many positive results of this move was to get Dr. Charles Mayo, a founder of the clinic, to lend his considerable influence to Brittin's hard work. The colonel also brought airline service to the

One of history's first pilots—Orville Wright—signed Northwest pilot Speed Holman's flying license.

town of Bismarck, North Dakota. The people showed their appreciation by naming the airport Brittin Field.

As part of his goodwill effort, Brittin offered help in planning and laying out airports throughout Minnesota. His next step was to give sight-seeing trips over the Twin Cities, using off-duty Northwest pilots. (The author of this book was on one of those flights in 1928.) Later the same year, Brittin accomplished a miracle when he talked six different railroads into getting together to combine rail and air service. And in one well-photographed operation, he had one of his planes backed up near a railroad car to transfer mail! Because aerial navigation was still difficult at night, the trains took care of business in the dark, and the planes flew during sunlight.

For the first few years of his work for Northwest, Colonel Brittin did not receive a salary. His pay came from the St. Paul Association, but, finally, he was brought into the company, given the title "manager," and paid $1,000 a month. About the same time, he began using the Ford Tri-motor, which had both pilot and copilot, carried 14 passengers, flew 125 miles per hour, and even had a toilet. Now, as an officer of the airline, he hired Charles Lindbergh as a consultant— not only a good idea in itself, but also very good publicity. And the post office extended its mail contract to Northwest from five to seven days a week.

Late in 1929, Brittin, always pushing forward, got his airline into night flights. At this time, ownership of

Minneapolis-St. Paul assistant postmaster C.L. Smith congratulates Northwest pilot Leon DeLong on the first night airmail flight between the Twin Cities and Chicago.

the business moved to the Twin Cities, due to his tireless efforts to get the business people there into the company through stock purchases. Now the line showed its first monthly profit, and Brittin was made a vice-president, not just because of the profit, but because of his enormous contributions in all phases of the operation.

Trying to make his planes and pilots look first class and be different from competitors, Brittin designed an insignia to be worn on the shirts of the pilots. (This was the forerunner of the wings now worn by pilots of all airlines.) He also put his pilots into uniforms, the very first line to do so. And the wings of all Northwest planes now carried the words *U.S. Airmail.* The colonel made his presence felt everywhere. He was, his people said, a "nut" for things being in order, and he insisted that hangar floors be swept every day and all workers wear coveralls. Such simple disciplines are standard today, but in those early times, they made Northwest look unique and very special in an industry that was still struggling.

Brittin also led the way for the entire industry by setting up a radio network to get weather information for the pilots. Until then, pilots got their own weather news by picking up the phone and calling ahead to the city to which they were flying! Brittin also plugged for expansion, not only into small towns in Minnesota, but also into Wisconsin, North Dakota, Montana, and

Pilots have Lewis Brittin to thank for designing the wings emblem they proudly wear.

Washington. The big airlines of that time, like United, got most of the good assignments from the post office, which was a powerful government agency. In a literal sense, the postmaster general was a dictator who could not only award mail contracts, but could also tell any airline *where* to fly, whether doing so was profitable or not.

Given this obstacle, Brittin looked for any possible way to increase business and even bought two amphibians (flying boats) to land on Lake Superior and serve the city of Duluth. He worked hardest on his main goal—to put a route across the northern United States. He got the support of business leaders in North Dakota, Montana, and Washington, and he began to spend more and more time in Washington, D.C.

Finally, after months of effort, the post office gave Northwest permission to fly to Bismarck, the capital of North Dakota. A few weeks later, Brittin installed a two-way radio in all his planes. When his chief pilot, "Speed" Holman, was killed in a crash in Omaha (at an air show), he replaced him with another man who, shortly after, died during an operation. Brittin shook off these setbacks, got a new chief pilot, and over the next several months, the airline began to make significant profits.

In 1932, Amelia Earhart, the famous American pilot, flew solo across the Atlantic. Her flight generated more favorable publicity for aviation and for Northwest, for which she was a consultant. Brittin was now spending

100 percent of his time in Washington, D.C., and was given his first bonus, $1,000, for his continued effective work. His main goal was still the northern route, and Brittin arranged for a flight with Amelia Earhart, himself, and several business people to fly the route in the dead of winter. Accomplished ahead of schedule, this resulted in much favorable publicity. Two days before Franklin Roosevelt took office as president of the United States, the postmaster gave Northwest approval to fly the northern route.

But a new and enormous problem lay ahead. Northwest's board had just approved purchase of the new Lockheed 10-A Electras, which could fly at 215 miles per hour. But a few days later, President Roosevelt told his postmaster to halt all further new routes and to cancel all mail contracts: the U.S. Army Air Corps would now fly the mail! This proved to be a dreadful decision.

After dozens of crashes and deaths, Roosevelt reversed the order and private airlines again began flying mail. Now Brittin continued to work tirelessly to get the full northern route to Seattle, Washington. Finally, approval came! For the moment, Brittin was an even larger hero to the company than at any time in the past. However, an event was about to take place that would have a major effect on his career.

Many airlines at this time were involved in *interlocking ownership*. Under this arrangement, some airlines and aircraft manufacturers owned large amounts of each other's stock. Because of this, the airlines involved would give preferential treatment to the manufacturing company that they owned stock in. Moreover, the manufacturers would, in turn, provide airplanes at lower prices to their own airlines than to competitors such as Brittin and Northwest. Brittin, believing this arrangement unfair, pressured government to break up the interlocking ownerships. He wrote a long account of the problem, so detailed that if it fell into unfriendly hands, it could hurt him, even though he had done nothing illegal or unethical.

A famous radio commentator of the time, Fulton Lewis, Jr., broke the story that the U.S. Postal Service had awarded Eastern Airlines a mail contract even though its bid was much higher than a small competitor. This news caused panic throughout the industry. Government investigators, sensing other problems, broke into the offices of several major airlines and seized all papers they found. Brittin tore up his detailed memo, not wanting it in the government's hands. For this action, he was accused of contempt of Congress and later spent ten days in jail.

Not wanting any harm to come to his beloved airline, Brittin immediately resigned. At age 57, he became a consultant on aviation matters until he died, at 75. During these years, he was a productive member of the business community and the aviation industry.

Colonel Brittin spent just seven years with Northwest. Others followed him, including some very fine executives. But he is the one who set Northwest on a course that has helped make it, today, the fourth largest U.S. airline.

In 1926, a few days before it began as a business, Northwest Airways had no planes. Nearly 70 years later, Northwest Airlines is a giant, with more than 300 airplanes that fly to destinations in more than 20 countries on 4 continents—Asia, Europe, Australia, and North America. In every sense of the word, Colonel Lewis Brittin became an American success story. Although not as well known as others in this book, his accomplishments were enormous. And he has earned a high rank not only in the history of American aviation, but also in the business world in general. Colonel Brittin was a truly extraordinary person!

Young L.L. Bean turned his love for hunting and fishing into a company that made the outdoors more enjoyable for millions.

2

L.L. Bean:
The Outdoorsman Who
Hated Wet Feet

*T*he small town of Freeport, Maine, is home to one of the most unusual businesses in the world. Freeport is the home of L.L. Bean, Inc., the largest outdoor specialty company in the world. In 1991, Bean's sales were more than $600 million; in the big holiday period before Christmas, the company employs 5,000 people.

Bean carries more than 5,500 different items and sells most of them through catalogs distributed in North America. In a recent year, the company mailed more than 114 million catalogs and shipped more than 11 million packages. In just one day, Bean sent out 125,000 items; in one busy week, 612,000. The fascinating Bean retail store in Freeport is open 7 days a week, 24 hours a day—even Christmas!

The Bean name is not as famous as General Motors or Disney, but one household out of every five in America has a product with a Bean logo—a pair of the original hunting boots that made Bean so well known or something more recent, like a pair of sunglasses or running shorts.

Leon Leonwood Bean was born in the mountains of western Maine in 1872. Although he died in 1967 at age 94, most Bean customers think of the company as just one man, one who still loves the outdoors and makes good products. Undoubtedly this highly personal image is the heart of the company's success and makes Bean today a special company in a special business.

Bean became an orphan at age 12 and had to fend for himself early in life. As a young boy, he worked on farms doing odd jobs and also earned a little money trapping, and selling soap from door to door. Although he was a natural salesman, he was never really satisfied in one job and drifted about from place to place. Finally, he settled in a Freeport dry goods store his brother owned. (A dry goods store in those days had mostly work clothing and helpful things for the home.) Paid $12 a week, Bean sold overalls to men who did manual labor.

In his spare time, Bean hunted and fished, and on every trip into the woods, he experienced the problem of wet feet, as did most hunters. Returning from one deer hunt, he complained about the discomfort and decided to do something about it.

Bean decided to take an ordinary pair of galoshes and sew leather tops on them. Then he would have the best of both worlds—the protection of rubber bottoms and the comfort and good fit of leather. When the boots were ready, he went hunting in them. He called this "field testing," which is what he would later do with all the products he sold.

Not much to look at and not as sturdy as L.L. thought they should be, the new boots did keep his feet dry. He figured that if the boot worked for him, it would work for others, and maybe he could get a little business going on the side. So he asked a local shoe-maker to produce a few pairs of these boots, and then he wrote a letter telling about what he called "The Maine Hunting Shoe." He mailed the letter to all the men who had bought Maine hunting licenses. In the letter, he wrote that the boot was "light as a moccasin, with the protection of a heavy hunting boot."

Simple and clear, the letter showed the promise of young L.L. as an effective writer of advertising copy. In the mail-order business, the ability to write well and to provide facts in an interesting style is very important, and Bean was just naturally good at it. His letter also pointed out that the boot was "the lightest made" and that it came in whole and half sizes. It was also, he wrote, "the lowest price of any sporting shoe on the market, at just $3.50 a pair."

Bean then added an idea of pure genius, an idea that would become the foundation of the company he would

At his Freeport store in the 1950s, L.L. Bean offers the famous Maine Hunting Shoe to a customer.

later found—the written guarantee. Not only would his company deliver the boots at no extra cost, but if buyers were not satisfied with them, they could also return them and Bean would refund the money.

The little brochure that accompanied the letter was a marvel of copy writing because of its simplicity. Unlike other catalogs of the time, it did not contain long-winded descriptions. Potential buyers knew that a person who really hunted and who understood hunter's needs and special problems had written this brochure. In addition to offering a guarantee, Bean delivered each pair of boots with a small repair kit to fix snags and rips.

The whole idea, conceived by a person of little experience, was outstanding. And the natural skill that Bean showed in his advertising writing has held over to this very day in the famous Bean catalog, which experts in advertising view as one of the best.

Was Bean's idea a huge success from the beginning? No. Of the first 100 pairs he sold, buyers returned 90 because the leather tops tended to separate from the rubber bottoms. But L.L. Bean preferred to do things right. Rather than go back on his promise, he refunded every dollar and then went to work to determine how to improve the boots. He had, after all, guaranteed every pair, and to him, a guarantee was a rock-solid promise.

The cover of a Bean Christmas catalog

So, Bean took a pair of the boots to Boston, where he met with people at U.S. Rubber Company. Together, they developed a boot that matched his original idea. Then he borrowed money to produce the boot in quantity. He sent out more letters and brochures, and of course, he offered his guarantee. But this time he added another smart idea and made the guarantee "unconditional." That is, a customer could return the boot at any time and for any reason and get a replacement or money back.

L.L. Bean has offered this unconditional guarantee ever since. If a customer wears or uses one of Bean's products for a year, two years, even three or more, and doesn't like it, the buyer can get his or her money back! A fisherman who bought a Bean rod and broke off the tip through his own carelessness brought it in for repair and to his amazement got a brand-new rod. Later, a man borrowed this rod and broke it. When he brought it in for repair, the clerk told him that Bean would replace the rod. "Bean stands by its products," said the salesperson.

L.L. Bean has always stood for Maine honesty and for the quality of its products. When the bottoms of an original hunting boot wore out after many years of tracking in the forests and stepping over sharp rocks, Bean would sew on new bottoms for just $3.10. And Bean still does this today, although of course the cost is higher.

When he got the hunting boot to the level of quality

he wanted, L.L. discussed with his brother the idea of going into the mail-order business. He moved across the street from the dry goods store and set up his business. He added knit stockings to the line and then additional outdoor gear.

By 1924, Bean was doing $135,000 in volume per year and employed 25 people. In 1927, he put fishing and camping equipment into the catalog. In his advertising copy, he wrote, "It is no longer necessary for you to experiment with hundreds of flies to determine the few that will catch fish. We have done that experimenting for you." Over and above the catalog itself, word-of-mouth advertising built the business to greater sales volume every year.

When a customer wrote to complain about an item, Bean wrote back, often enclosing a gift and sometimes inviting the person on a fishing trip. To L.L., every customer was a real person—to be dealt with honestly and fairly. He reinvested most of the profit the little business began to make. He built the mailing list, ran hundreds of small ads in outdoor magazines, and offered a free catalog.

By 1934, although the country was deep in the Great Depression, Bean had doubled its dollar volume of ten years earlier, then doubled it again. Instead of putting the profit into his pocket, L.L. invested nearly every dollar he made back into the business, with his eye on building it for the long term.

As the business grew, L.L. served on the school

L.L. Bean's original store in the 1930s

board and helped attract new businesses to Maine. He became active in various outdoor organizations, which were not nearly as popular then as they are today. His way of doing business continued throughout his career.

Bean often got phone calls in the middle of the night from fishermen who were in town and wanted equipment and advice. One night, when he was in his eighties, Bean got such a call. He went to the store, sold the fishermen what they wanted, and then decided to keep his store open 24 hours a day, every day.

36

Throughout his life, L.L. kept expanding the catalog, making it better and better, adding more and more merchandise, putting millions more people on his mailing lists. Direct-mail advertising is terribly expensive, but to a business like Bean, it is their life blood. His catalogs were so interesting, so well done, so filled with pictures and stories of Bean merchandise that customers eagerly looked forward to having a copy come to their home. As orders began to pour in for various Bean products, L.L. established another policy that would remain until 1990—all merchandise sent to customers was postage-paid; that is, Bean, not the customer, paid for delivery.

Successful as Bean's business was, however, and popular as he himself had become, dark clouds loomed on the horizon as he became older. A small number of his top managers could see problems that were beginning to affect the health of the company. No longer did annual sales increase 25 percent or more each year; dollar volume actually began to flatten. Merchandise in the catalog and in the store was no longer up-to-the-minute, and even worse, orders were being slowly filled by part-time people who had little interest in doing the best possible job. With these and other problems in mind, two or three of L.L.'s employees approached him, urging changes to improve the business and maybe even to save it. But he usually responded by saying, "I'm eating three meals a day now, and I can't eat four." This attitude, as logical as it sounds, did not help a faltering company. Nor did it satisfy the employees who raised the point. Also, at this time, more and more competitors were moving into the sports specialty field. Given this, the employees thought that the business that L.L. had founded and run so well for so long would shrivel up and disappear.

But this didn't happen. Why? Because of Leon Gorman, grandson of L.L., who became president of the company in 1967. Leon, born in New Hampshire, got his college degree from Bowdoin and went to work in Filene's, a large department store in Boston. Then he went into the navy, where he spent four years on a destroyer. When discharged, he went to work for the company his grandfather founded; his salary was $80 a week.

Because Leon's own business experience was limited, the most logical way of working was to learn as much as he could from his grandfather. The principles of L.L. became Leon's principles. He believed, as his grandfather did, that a company should personally test a product before selling it and that a good business gives complete customer satisfaction. He learned to write advertising copy, and he followed L.L.'s conservative methods of handling money. Nor could he fail to be strongly influenced by the old man's strong personality and honesty.

Although the powerful Bean image had helped the company succeed, L.L. had run the business as a one-person show, not delegating responsibility, nor, even worse, laying any plans for the future. To Leon's credit, he recognized the problems even though he had little business experience. He studied the old catalogs, talked to old-time employees, and spent many hours asking questions of the salespeople who sold merchandise to the company. Although not as avid an outdoorsman as L.L., he became involved in hunting and fishing, and he took evening courses in business at the University of Maine in Portland.

In the mid- and late 1960s, a recreation boom was going on in the United States. People had more money, more leisure time, and they began to look to the out-of-doors for fun and exercise as well as for family togetherness. Camping and backpacking became major activities, and young adults started wearing sports apparel and footwear. All of this could be good for Bean's business, but unless they were ready to take advantage of the interest in nature, only their competitors would benefit.

In late 1967, L.L. Bean died, and more than 50,000 letters of sympathy arrived at the the company headquarters in Freeport, Maine. Many of the letter writers requested catalogs. This proved that the company had a fundamental strength if grandson Leon could revitalize it. What Leon did was take the basic L.L. Bean image and bring it up to date. He made prices more competitive and added both a summer and a Christmas catalog. He continued to advertise in outdoor magazines, but added general interest magazines to broaden Bean's market appeal. And, he did one additional thing that

Leon Gorman successfully used modern business practices to expand the market for Bean's products.

companies in trouble seldom do—he *increased* the advertising budget!

Next, Leon added hundreds of thousands of names to the catalog mailing list. The first year under Leon's direction, annual sales went up 25 percent and hit nearly $5 million. By 1975, annual sales reached $30 million, and more than 400 people worked for the company in Freeport. The company answered every customer complaint, and the retail store in Freeport put in higher-quality merchandise, increased the selection, and still maintained the friendly northwoods atmosphere.

Leon recognized another problem and moved quickly to solve it. As sales increased, the other end of the business—that of filling the orders and properly managing the large inventory of products—was falling behind because of old and inefficient handling procedures.

To improve the handling of orders, Leon computerized many segments of the business that up until then had been done with the bare hands of employees, often with poor results. He moved the manufacturing plant into a new building, which resulted in better and faster production with less wasted time. He increased pay levels and put in programs for job-ratings and performance bonuses. He added pension, savings, and group life insurance and provided professional training courses for supervisors. (In 1990, more than 3,000 Bean employees attended what Leon called "Total Quality" sessions, a program to produce excellence in all phases of service and operation.) Working conditions vastly improved, and people of unusual merit could now advance in the company.

Equally important, Leon Gorman ran the company with a watchful eye on spending, and the company had no debt. Technology and the L.L. Bean image may not seem to fit together, but intelligently applied by Leon Gorman, technology saved the business and helped it grow to more than $600 million in sales.

When L.L. was still alive and his company successful, he wrote, "A chief reason for the success of the business is that I tried on the trail every article I sell. If I tell you a knife is good for cleaning trout, it is because I

The company's 90,000 square foot retail store, on Main Street in Freeport, Maine, sits on the site of L.L. Bean's original store.

personally found it so." L.L.'s company has become famous all over the world, and L.L. himself is still beloved by outdoors people everywhere. Many famous people have been Bean customers—presidents Calvin Coolidge and Franklin Roosevelt, baseball player Ted Williams, heavyweight boxing champ Jack Dempsey, movie star John Wayne, and Lowell Thomas, the celebrated TV and radio news personality.

In the early 1980s, the company made huge gains in so-called "preppie" merchandise that appealed to well-educated young men and women who had a taste for clothing with style and usefulness. When this part of the business began to fall off in 1983, the company went back to basics. It also become deeply involved in environmental issues, working closely with groups such as the Nature Conservancy and Ducks Unlimited. The original L.L. Bean was an outdoorsman with an instinct for business, and Leon Gorman, his grandson, is a sound business person who has developed an intense interest in the out-of-doors.

The Bean guarantee was the original basic idea, and Gorman has kept it alive. In addition, he has installed sound business methods and intelligent treatment of employees. L.L. Bean, Inc., founded in 1912, is today by far the leading seller of outdoor specialty merchandise in the world. And the image of the nice old outdoorsman up in Maine is still the thought that is in the heads of Bean customers.

Walt Disney adjusts his movie camera, the tool he would use so well to gain worldwide fame and fortune.

3

Walt Disney:
And a Mouse That Might Have
Been Named Mortimer

*B*orn in Chicago in 1901, Walter Elias Disney moved with his family to a farm in Missouri when he was only four, so he always considered himself a small-town boy. On the farm, he loved the animals and learned to draw them. He had three older brothers and a sister, and the boys worked hard doing farm work.

Their father, a stern man who also worked as a carpenter to support the family, did not believe in paying his children to do work for the family. So, when two of the older brothers got enough money together, they left home for good. In 1910, Walt's father was stricken with typhoid fever but recovered. He was unable, however, to work the farm, so he sold it and moved the family to Kansas City. There, he bought a paper route, and

45

young Walt delivered papers at no pay. But Walt never felt sorry for himself and never got discouraged.

In high school, Walt became an actor of sorts and once came to school dressed as Abraham Lincoln. He delivered the Gettysburg Address to delighted classmates. But he liked drawing best, and when he graduated, his cartoons appeared in the class books of his friends.

When Walt's father returned to Chicago, Walt stayed in Kansas City for the summer and sold candy on the Santa Fe Railroad. Typically, however, he spent most of what he earned, and when he went back to Chicago to join the family, he didn't have a dime left of his summer earnings. In Chicago, he went to art school three nights a week and drew cartoons in his spare time.

During World War I, Walt wanted to enlist in the army, but, being too young, he joined the Red Cross as an ambulance driver. He spent his spare time in Europe drawing cartoons and sending them back to various magazines in the United States. When Walt returned to Chicago a year later, he worked for an art studio that made advertisements for farm magazines, but the studio soon went bankrupt. Walt then took a job with the Kansas City Slide Company making cartoon commercials for local businesses. Now, for the first time, people could actually see Walt's cartoons because they were shown to theater audiences along with the feature movie.

Walt loved this business. The world of animation

Young Kansas City cartoonist Walt Disney works at the craft he would later perfect in Hollywood.

was just beginning to take hold and become popular with movie-goers. Walt and a friend named Ubbe Iwwerks from Holland worked hard to become good at the technique and spent hours at the library reading about the science of animation. Walt even created some experimental comics, which he called "Laugh-O-Grams," and although he wasn't making any significant money, he was learning. He also enjoyed knowing that his work was being seen.

With the $500 he got for doing a cartoon film for a local dentist, Walt bought a camera. He made a deal with a film company to do a number of cartoons for the

A struggling artist, Walt created this newspaper advertisement to attract business.

huge sum of $11,000, but the deal fell through. When that happened, he sold the camera, packed his suitcase, and left for Hollywood. The year was 1923.

In California, Walt lived with an uncle and set up a studio in the garage. He made arrangements to sell six cartoons he called *Alice's Wonderland*. Then he persuaded his older brother Roy to come in and run the financial part of the business. Roy, who was smart with dollars, offered a good balance to Walt, who was highly creative and never worried about money.

The two brothers started Disney Brothers Studio, rented a tiny office, bought a used camera, and hired two assistants. But they had only one set of decent clothing between them, so they could go out to look for business only one at a time. And they were so poor that they bought one lunch at the cafeteria and shared it. They saved by living together in a tiny apartment, where they argued and got on each other's nerves.

As business slowly improved, Walt brought his old friend Ubbe from Kansas City to help do the animation and hired a secretary, Lillian Bounds, to help in the office. (Lillian was later to become Mrs. Walt Disney.) In 1924, Charlie Mintz, who worked in the film distribution business in New York, bought eight *Alice* cartoons for $1,500 apiece. The deal sounded good, but the small company always had trouble getting paid on time. However, by 1925, the business was growing.

Walt and his early partner, Ubbe Iwwerks

49

The Disney family outside their Los Angeles studio. From left: Lillian, Walt, sister Ruth, Roy, and Edna, Roy's wife.

Roy married, and he and Walt bought a piece of property in Hollywood for a studio that had an office for each of them. But, as in the past, nothing came easily. Constantly behind in his payments, Charlie Mintz ordered more *Alice* cartoons in 1926 but insisted he could not pay as much as before. Walt was now drawing less often and working more at managing the artists he had. In addition, he was the idea person.

The brothers changed the name of the business to Walt Disney Productions because they knew people liked to think that a single person did the drawing of the cartoons.   Then Universal Pictures asked for a new series built around a rabbit, and Walt created Oswald the Lucky Rabbit, a character that caught on with movie fans.   Now, with a real star going for them, the brothers obtained more studio space.   Payments for each Oswald episode jumped to $2,250.

But then came real disaster, the kind of problem that would stay with Walt, more or less, for the rest of his life.   Charlie Mintz, instead of giving them a new contract, hired all Walt's animators behind his back and left

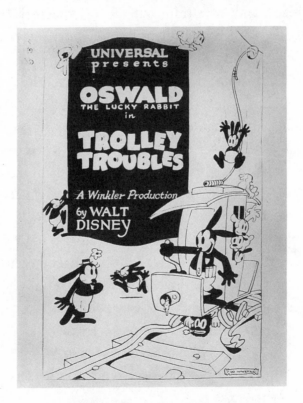

Oswald the Lucky Rabbit, Walt's 1927 creation with Universal Pictures, was his first popular cartoon character.

Walt with nothing, not even Oswald. Oswald, said Mintz, belonged to him, and legally, this was true. Now Walt and Roy had nothing. Back to square one!

The experience with Mintz was Walt's first with the vicious nature of show business. He was crushed. More than anything else, he expected loyalty from those with whom he worked, and to think that animators who worked with him would leave, and particularly under such circumstances, outraged and saddened him.

Nevertheless, one of Walt's greatest qualities was optimism, and on a train trip from New York back to California with wife Lillian, he got out paper and pen and began to draw. Taking shape on paper was a new character, a mouse wearing clothes. When he had him about right, Walt turned to Lillian and asked, "What do you think of the name 'Mortimer'?" His wife, not liking the name Mortimer at all, suggested Mickey, and thus began one of the greatest success stories in all history!

Back in California, Walt and Ubbe Iwwerks (the only artist who had not deserted him) developed the character and began working to turn out their first mouse cartoon. They released two Mickey cartoons in 1928, and audiences loved them. At about the same time, sound came to the movies (which in the past had always been silent). Singer Al Jolson had made a "talkie" called *The Jazz Singer*, and when Walt saw it, he immediately saw that sound would totally change the film industry forever.

Always an innovator, and with shrewd instincts, Walt

never lacked the courage to try something new. So he reworked the two Mickey cartoons and made them adaptable for sound. The studio hired musicians, and Walt became Mickey's voice. When Disney's newest film, *Steamboat Willie*, hit the theaters in New York, the audience was wild about it, far more so than for the feature film with which it ran.

Suddenly, Mickey Mouse cartoons were popular, and Walt made a deal with Pat Powers, a distributor from New York who offered $2,500 a film. Brother Roy did not like the contract because it gave too much to Pat Powers, and he did not trust the man. But Walt, hating negative thoughts, plunged ahead, hired four more animators, and got a contract for ten new Mickey films.

Walt gave Ubbe a 20 percent share in the studio and put his name on the film credits, in gratitude for his loyalty and good work. Now, finally, Walt could relax a little, but this was not his style and never would be. He began to create a new kind of cartoon, which he called *Silly Symphonies*. Here he set animation to classical music. The cartoon did not rely on funny gags. The first of these films featured dancing skeletons, which were developed by Ubbe. It wowed the critics in a test showing, and is an all-time classic even today.

However, lack of money continued to be a problem. The checks from Pat Powers were not what they should have been, and Walt sent Roy to New York to investigate. Roy found, as he had suspected, that Powers was a crook who wanted to own the Disney ideas himself.

Mickey Mouse at the helm in Steamboat Willie

Powers next tried to hire Walt at the huge salary of $130,000 a year. Walt, not wanting to work for anyone, refused. Then the crafty Powers hired Ubbe, who sold his share of the studio back to the brothers for $2,920. (Years later, this share would have been worth many millions of dollars!) Many years later, Ubbe returned to work for Disney, but his departure to Pat Powers made Walt realize that never again should he let any individual person become so important that his leaving would hurt the company. From that time on the company name became "Walt Disney." Walt said "the company is Walt Disney. That Walt Disney is not even me. I drink and smoke. That is not the company. The company is bigger than any one person, and even I am not Walt Disney anymore." Walt saw that "Disney" was not even a group of people. It was a thing, an image.

By 1930, Walt was 29 and had 75 employees. He worked all the time, smoked constantly, and got little sleep. His wife had lost two children in childbirth and the stress of his work and home life took its toll. His doctor sent him on a long trip and then proposed he take up some hobbies. First, he tried golf, but it made him furious. Then he took up polo.

By 1932, Walt was somewhat better and still filled with enthusiasm and dozens of new ideas. The Great Depression was hurting most of the country, but, strangely, these hard times were good for Walt's business because people went to the movies to forget their troubles. Most films were either horror, gangster or comedies, with the Marx Brothers or Charlie Chaplin, whom Walt admired greatly.

Then color came to the movies. Walt learned of a company called "Technicolor" that had developed a new product. He ordered production stopped on a current cartoon and had it converted to color. Roy, in charge of the money, objected, and the two fought.

Walt understood Roy's value to the studio, but also knew that he, Walt, was the better judge of quality. He never wanted money to stand in the way of Disney films being the absolute best. Roy finally gave in, but only if the studio could get an exclusive contract. Walt agreed, and for two years, *Silly Symphonies* were the only cartoons in color. The studio's first all-color film, *Flowers and Trees*, won an Academy Award.

With new fame and success, Walt could now hire all

Although Roy argued with Walt, each brother's skills—Roy's financial and Walt's artistic—complemented the other's.

the animators he wanted. Because of the Depression, many of them were willing to work for little or nothing. He constantly taught his staff how to do things better and hired instructors to help improve the quality of the drawings. He wanted a plot, or story line, in every cartoon, and he created the concept of *storyboards* so that animators could work out the plot before beginning the animation. He insisted that all the animals in his cartoons have real character, and he brought in live deer, lambs, and squirrels and made his artists observe them. The animators watched and studied and then drew.

Walt ponders the storyboards that cover the hallway walls of his studio.

In 1933, Walt and his wife, Lillian, finally had a child, Diane. That same year, he finished *The Three Little Pigs,* with its popular song, "Who's Afraid of the Big Bad Wolf?"

Now, Walt plunged ahead with another new and expensive idea—the first full-length cartoon film, *Snow White.* This project cost far more money than the studio had, and Disney borrowed more than $1 million to complete the film. When it opened in Los Angeles in 1937, it was a smash hit. Many movie stars of the day came to see it, and the critics raved about its quality.

Scenes from two animated Disney film classics: Snow White, *released in 1937, and* Bambi *(bottom), released in 1942.*

Next, the studio finished the films *Pinocchio* and *Bambi*. Both were immediately successful, but Walt reinvested the money the studio took in from these successes right back into the business. He was always building, always innovating, always demanding better quality. Many of the artists objected and demanded higher pay.

Walt, interested only in better work, became a demanding tyrant. He criticized people in front of others, screamed, and tore up work he thought badly done. He hated laziness and thought many of his employees were taking things too easy, staying too long at lunch, not caring enough about their work. Trying to offset this, he regularly brought in famous people like architect Frank Lloyd Wright and writer Alexander Woollcott to inspire the artists to greatness.

Because a war had begun in Europe, the studio's business from there fell off considerably. The government of the United States decided that certain materials the studio was using for sound reproduction were needed for the war effort and cut off these materials from Disney.

Despite its success, *Pinocchio* had not made enough money to pay for its huge costs and the costs of other films. Rumors spread that the company was in trouble and that layoffs would follow. In order to bring in more money and to give his employees a share in the business, Walt decided to sell stock in the company. His scheme didn't work. When the animators went on strike in

1941, Walt felt betrayed. He later said that this was the toughest time of his life.

In the autumn of 1941, the studio released *Dumbo*, the story of a flying elephant, which became a huge hit. But when the Japanese attacked the U.S. naval base at Pearl Harbor, the army took possession of Walt's studio because it was next door to the Lockheed aircraft plant, which would be needed to manufacture many warplanes. Now, with the United States at war, the studio began to make films for the military. The most famous was *Der Fuehrer's Face*, which won an Academy Award in 1943.

Still, by the end of the war, the studio was again deeply in debt. Walt wanted to move ahead with new projects; Roy wanted to get things under control before spending more money. They had violent arguments. Finally, Walt won one argument and did a film about seals. *Seal Island* won an Academy Award. This was the beginning of a new company, True Life Adventure films, which was successful and profitable.

At age 46, Walt, always fascinated by trains, built a miniature train system on his property and began to dream about an amusement park. This, of course, would cost huge amounts of money, and he had just spent $250,000 to reshoot a storm scene completely for his film *Twenty Thousand Leagues under the Sea*.

To help him establish the amusement park, Walt started a small company called WED (Walt E. Disney) for special projects. He took complete control. His researchers found a place in Anaheim, California, to build the new park. It would cost millions of dollars, and where would the money come from? Walt knew—from a new medium called "television."

While most movie people were afraid of TV because they thought it would hurt their business, Walt saw it as a new opportunity for millions of people to see his films. Both CBS and NBC turned down his ideas. ABC, however, lent him $500,000 in return for a share in the studio. The first Disney production was a one-hour show in 1954, and his first big production was "Davy Crockett," which starred Fess Parker. The TV show

Fess Parker starred in Disney's first television series, "Davy Crockett."

The castle at Disneyland, the monument to Walt Disney's imagination that millions of visitors haveled traveled to since 1955.

was a huge hit. Then Walt did "Zorro," and a "Man in Space" episode (he did this five years before the U.S. government started its own space program).

With money now coming in from television, Walt plunged ahead with his amusement park, to be called "Disneyland." It opened in July 1955, and, while the opening day itself was a disaster because so many things went wrong, the new park ultimately was a success. Another huge success was "The Mickey Mouse Club" on TV with its female star, Mousketeer Annette Funicello. Now, with success after success coming to him and to the studio, Walt spent every minute working to make Disneyland better and better—better food, cleaner restrooms, friendlier employees.

At the same time, the studio was turning out successful films like *The Absentminded Professor*, with star Fred MacMurray, and *The Swiss Family Robinson*. In 1964, the studio released *Mary Poppins* with Julie. Andrews and Dick Van Dyke and *Pollyanna* with Haley Mills, who would do six Disney movies. Another animated film, *One Hundred and One Dalmatians*, was also wonderfully successful. After 40 years in business, Walt and Roy were finally out of debt, now rich and still fighting.

One of the very good moves that Walt and Roy made was to get together with a man who specialized in a type of promotion called *merchandising*. That is, they put Mickey Mouse's picture on all kinds of things, like pajamas, towels, wall paper, anything that kids would like and their parents would buy for them.

Walt now began looking for a second park and finally decided that Florida would be the best location. He wanted to build an ideal city of the future, where people could live and work—no slums, no crime, no pollution. He called his city "EPCOT" (Experimental Prototype Community of Tomorrow). As usual, he poured himself into this project with all his enthusiasm and brilliance. He did this in spite of the fact that he was in pain most of the time. He smoked and coughed constantly. His friends and associates began to comment on how bad he looked.

EPCOT Center visitors zoom past Spaceship Earth on their voyage to an imaginary world of the future (top), as a band in colonial costumes entertains tourists in Liberty Square at Walt Disney World, Florida's 27,000-acre amusement area.

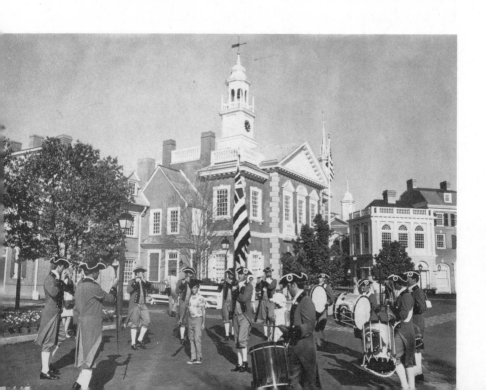

On New Year's Day, 1966, Walt was Grand Marshall of the Rose Bowl Parade. A short time later, he learned that he had lung cancer. Working with pain all day long, he moved ahead with the work on the Florida park, which would be called "Disney World." On December 15, 1967, he died.

Almost everyone thought that Disney World would also die without Walt. It finally opened, however, and has been successful ever since. The studio Walt founded has also produced several new animated films, including *Beauty and the Beast, The Little Mermaid, Aladdin,* and *The Lion King.*

Against the odds, what Walt Disney started and built is still very much alive. Today, Disney has 40,000 employees around the world. Tokyo Disneyland opened in 1983 and Euro Disneyland in 1992. In 1992, Lillian Disney gave $50 million for a Walt Disney Concert Hall in Los Angeles.

While Walt himself is gone, what he created, through his genius, his enthusiasm, and his determination to be the best always, is still here. And the mouse who could have been called "Mortimer" is surely the best-known animal in all the world!

Gifted writer Bruce Barton turned his flair for words into one of the world's largest advertising agencies.

4

Bruce Barton:
Advertising Genius

*B*ruce Barton, an extremely talented writer who wrote books and magazine articles, became an advertising person, a best-selling publisher, a member of the United States Congress, and an adviser to at least two presidents of the United States. Barton was born in Tennessee in 1886, the son of a minister father and a school teacher mother. In later years, Barton said, "We were not poor, we just didn't have any money."

His father moved the family to Oak Park, Illinois, where Bruce began work at an early age, selling newspapers when he was 9. At 16, he made $600 selling maple syrup. He became editor of his school paper, and his classmates voted him "Most Likely to Succeed." Barton entered Berea College in Kentucky, but later transferred to Amherst College in Massachusetts, from which he graduated in 1907. There he was elected to Phi Beta Kappa, a high academic honor. With jobs hard to get, he went to Montana to work in a construction camp ten hours a day for $60 a month.

Because he liked to write, Barton was offered a job back in Chicago as an editorial assistant. In 1907, he became editor of the magazine *Home Herald.* Some time later, he became editor of the magazine *Housekeeper. Collier's Weekly* magazine in New York then offered him a job as assistant sales manager.

One day, almost by accident, he wrote a small advertisement for the Harvard Classics series of books. His career as an advertising man was under way. In one successful ad, Barton wrote that readers who never attended college but who spent just 15 minutes a day with the Classics would nevertheless learn how to "think clearly, talk more convincingly, earn more and enjoy life more than many college men." His famous ads for the Classics sold more than 400,000 sets of books.

In 1913, Barton married and continued his writing career while raising a family. His writing made him well known all over the United States. Much of his writing consisted of essays, some with strong religious themes. Two of his most powerful works were "More Power to You" and "It's a Good Old World."

When the U.S. entered World War I, Bruce Barton volunteered his successful style of writing to the Salvation Army, for whom he wrote a slogan that became famous: "A man may be down, but he is never out." At the same time, he was also editor of the magazine *Every Week*. As a semi-celebrity, he was asked by the U.S. government to run the publicity for the United War Work Campaign.

Leading this volunteer group, Barton helped raise more than $200 million. During this period, he met two men, Alex Osborn and Roy Durstine, who persuaded him to join them in forming an advertising agency after the war. They agreed that he would be the creative chief of the agency, but that he could still write his magazine and newspaper articles.

The men borrowed $10,000 and opened for business in New York City in 1919. Barton wrote ads and looked for new clients. He proved very successful at this. He was tall and handsome and spoke well. However, on the first day of business, a major problem faced him. His key partner, Roy Durstine, became sick with pneumonia and was gone for three months. So Barton ran the business as well as wrote the ads. The new agency lost $50 the first week, but made a profit every week after that. "I was too ignorant to be scared," he later said. Years later, in talking about how the new agency had had no specialists or job descriptions, Barton said, "Every one of us knew what everyone else was doing."

With Barton doing most of the writing, and running the business, the agency grew. General Electric became one of the young firm's earliest big-name clients. The advertising agency then added a loosely connected manufacturer of automobiles, and Barton suggested that it

Barton's early partners, Alex Osborn (top) and Roy Durstine

be called "General Motors." For another client, General Mills, he created the name Betty Crocker as a symbol of the American homemaker. For U.S. Steel (a company that emerged from World War I with a bad reputation), he created an ad that said the company's founder, Andrew Carnegie, "came to a land of wooden towns and left a nation of steel." The ad helped to improve U.S. Steel's public reputation.

Dunlop Tire became a client, then Lever Brothers. For client Alexander Hamilton Institute, a correspondence school, Barton wrote an ad with the headline "The Years That the Locusts Have Eaten." In this ad, he sold the idea of hard work and told of the extra effort a person would need in order to study by mail at the end of a hard day's work at a regular job. He wrote another effective ad for the institute that ran for seven years, something unique in the advertising industry. The headline of this ad read, "About one man in ten will be appealed to by this page."

In 1923, Barton made a speech to a meeting of electric utility companies. In the speech, he warned that America kept producing new generations of people who did not know the difference between a Mazda lamp and a stick of Wrigley's gum. He pointed out, therefore, that advertising must be constantly applied. Years later, Barton's agency still got requests for copies of his speech, which was good publicity for the firm.

During the 1920s, Barton was the most famous advertising executive in the country. His capacity for writing was boundless, and even though he was deeply involved in all phases of his company's work, he found time to write a book (published in 1925) called *The Man Nobody Knows.* The book was about Jesus Christ, whom Barton saw as a great salesman. Barton wrote that "Christ picked up twelve men from the bottom ranks of business and forged them into an organization that conquered the world!" The highly controversial book led the best-seller lists in both the United States and England for two years! Later, Barton wrote a second book, *The Book Nobody Knows,* which was about the Bible. While this book was not a best seller as the first one had been, many people read it and talked about it.

As time went on, Bruce Barton proved to be one of

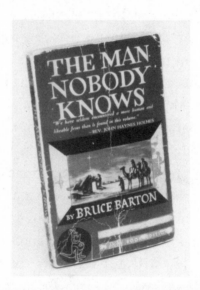

Barton's portrayal of Jesus in The Man Nobody Knows, *though praiseworthy, caused an uproar in some religious circles—and helped to make the book a best seller.*

the few advertising men who could not only manage a business, but could also write marvelous advertising copy for many different kinds of clients. In his ad campaign to help sell General Electric appliances, he wrote, "Any woman who does anything which a little electric motor can do is working for three cents an hour."

In 1928, an earlier advertising agency founded by George Batten merged with Barton and his partners. They called the new company Batten, Barton, Durstine & Osborn, or BBDO. One comedian joked that the new name sounded "like a bunch of suitcases falling down stairs."

This award-winning ad for General Electric, which became Barton's client in 1920, shows what a clever writer he was.

Now, with Barton as chairman, the new agency had billings of $32 million a year, a huge figure at that time. Over the next several years, BBDO grew to be one of the largest agencies in the entire world. Its many clients were some of the most famous companies on earth.

In spite of the record of what advertising can do for product sales, the business has always had its critics, particularly in the media. When two prominent writers of his day attacked the business, Barton retaliated in a widely publicized speech: "If advertising persuades some men to live beyond their means, so does matrimony. . . . If advertising is often . . . redundant and tiresome, so is the United States Senate."

When the firm founded by George Batten joined Barton, Durstine, and Osborn, their new agency took the name that became of one the most famous in the business—BBDO.

Barton liked ads that looked good; he liked clear and direct writing. During part of his career as an ad writer, he worked with Norman Rockwell, the famous artist of the *Saturday Evening Post* magazine. Barton would think up the ideas, and Rockwell would illustrate them.

On his office wall, Barton had a huge picture of a crowd of people at a popular beach. The picture, he felt, helped him to keep his audience in mind. "You're not talking to a mass meeting," Barton said. "You're writing ads to sweaty individuals." Addressing a group of clients, as agency people must do frequently to convince them of the wisdom of strong advertising campaigns, Barton would start slowly and hesitatingly. Then, with his audience quiet and leaning forward, he would make his points and hold them spellbound.

As BBDO and the advertising industry grew, the editor of a popular magazine of the time established a set of advertising awards. The Harvard Business School administered the awards so no one could accuse BBDO or other agencies of any kind of favoritism. During the years that these awards were presented, BBDO won twice as many as any other agency. This was not luck. Barton and his employees worked hard to be the best in their business. He said, "We are sitting in with manufacturers of cars and cabbages and sealing wax, and all of them have troubles which are passed on to us—and which we must regard as peculiarly personal and important."

In his own politics, Bruce Barton was a conservative

Seated in front of the mural that often inspired his writing, Barton meets with his 1957 management team. (Alex Osborn is at far left.)

Republican, believing in hard work, integrity, and careful handling of other people's money. Because of his articles and best-selling books, he was a famous person and, as such, was persuaded to run for Congress from his state of New York. In his first campaign, he told *The New York Times*, "I want to be known as the 'Great Repealer.' I will vote to repeal a law a week."

In 1940, President Franklin Roosevelt, who had begged Barton for his support but had never gotten it, lashed out, making fun of Barton. Roosevelt claimed that his greatest enemies in Congress were Joe Martin (Speaker of the House), Hamilton Fish of New York, and Barton. The president used his most heavy sarcasm in referring to the three men as some kind of fictitious advertising agency—"Martin, Barton . . . and Fish." The phrase caught on, made particularly memorable because of Roosevelt's considerable Eastern accent, so that the names came out "Mahton . . . Bahton . . . and Fish." This did nothing to harm Barton's already wide acceptance as an important public figure.

After two terms in Congress, Barton returned to BBDO and remained there until his retirement in 1961. As he grew older, his hair turned snow white, which made his looks even more striking. His manner of speech and his fame made him a widely sought public speaker. He had three children and two hobbies—reading ("above all else," he said) and golf. His library contained more than 1,000 books, all of which he had read, some of them many times.

Barton was a member of the First Congregational Church in Oak Park, Illinois, where his father had been minister. He was also president of the Institute for the Crippled and Disabled, trustee of the Columbia Medical College, national chairman of the United Negro College Fund, trustee of Berea College, and a member of many clubs. In 1957, he won the Franklin Award for distinguished service, given by the New York Employing Printers Association. In the same year, his college, Amherst, gave him an honorary degree.

Bruce Barton and his associates at BBDO wrote advertisements for many of the world's most famous companies—and the company continues to do so. BBDO's clients today include Diet Pepsi (with Ray Charles and the "Uh Huh" girls), Apple Computer, Delta Airlines, Polaroid, Dodge, Pillsbury, Burger King, Pizza Hut, Campbell's Soup Company, Gillette, and Wrigley's.

When Barton retired as head of BBDO, it was the fourth largest advertising agency in the world. It was Bruce Barton, probably as much as any one person, who created the "pictures" of products and corporations in a manner we now refer to as "image."

In the early 1990s, BBDO created the Diet Pepsi "Performance" commercial starring singer Ray Charles.

As an ad-man, Barton came in for criticism. But as the most famous advertising person of his day, he also had the huge support of his industry. Millions of people admired his writing and his courage. When he won the Gold Medal Award from *Printers' Ink* magazine, he was described as follows: "When judging the contributions a man has made in his lifetime, it is necessary to evaluate more than his achievements in his chosen business. Bruce Barton has served more than the advertising industry. Both he and advertising have served well all of the people of the United States. The public service Mr. Barton has rendered in Washington and elsewhere makes him a logical choice for the Gold Medal."

Bruce Barton, in retirement, maintained an office in New York and continued to write until his death in 1967. By all standards of measurement, he was a giant in the business of advertising and, as a writer and citizen, had a positive effect on the lives of millions of people.

Canadian Nathan Cummings, who began his career in the footwear business, built a huge multi-national corporation that acquired companies as often as most people bought new shoes.

5

Nathan Cummings:
"Nobody Doesn't Like Sara Lee"

*T*he Sara Lee Corporation is the biggest company in the world with a woman's name. That alone makes it different, but Sara Lee is different in dozens of ways from any other business anywhere. Sara Lee stands not only for coffee cake, but also for hundreds of products and a unique way of doing business.

Nathan Cummings started this amazing company. He was born in 1896 in Saint John, New Brunswick, Canada. His parents, immigrants from Lithuania, were poor. Nathan attended school in Canada, but the family needed money, so he dropped out of school and went to work in a shoe factory. He worked in the shoe business for several years, except for a short time spent in New York, where an uncle taught him how to dress a retail store window. There he learned a few basics of retail merchandising. By then, his father had started a shoe store, where Nathan worked until 1917. He liked the shoe business and was good at it, even then showing promise of becoming successful.

Soon, Nathan started his own shoe business, making a white summer shoe that he felt would sell well. But one day, soot from a passing train ruined the shoes he had made. With nothing to sell and no more money, he went bankrupt. He then went to work selling anything he could get his hands on. As he began to make and save a little money, he paid off all the debt of his bankruptcy, even though the bankruptcy laws said he did not have to do that.

In 1930, married and starting a family, Nathan moved from Canada to the United States. He had heard about a small company in Baltimore called "C.D. Kenny." It imported coffee and tea and distributed other food products. The business, which was not well run, was in danger of going bankrupt. Cummings, learning that a Baltimore credit company was in charge of trying to make the Kenny company healthy, convinced them that he was the person with the skills and determination to get the job done. And he did. Some years later, when he had helped to make the company successful, he bought it, becoming the owner in 1939. Cummings brought tough management methods to the little business, and through huge energy and smart street savvy, he made it grow. In 1945, to be closer to major food distribution centers, he moved the company

Nathan Cummings with daughter, Beatrice, and wife, Ruth

to Chicago and changed its name. The name "C.D. Kenny" didn't tell people much about what the company did, so he now called it "Consolidated Grocers Corporation." Then he arranged for the company's stock to be listed on the New York Stock Exchange.

Sometime during this period, Cummings conceived the idea of growing larger by purchasing other companies. Today, this is called "a strategy of acquisition," but back then, the idea had no name. Cummings learned how to make offers to owners of other businesses at just the right time, when those owners were only too happy to take the money and leave their troubles behind. As early as 1945, Cummings's business had become what today is called a *conglomerate*, which is one company made up of several different parts. He again changed the name, this time to Consolidated Foods Corporation, a name that was more descriptive than the previous ones. What he did then was the forerunner of a major trend in big business today. Cummings gathered together many different kinds of companies under one central management and ownership.

The idea was new, but Nathan made it work. The company, which today is known as Sara Lee Corporation, is probably the most diversified business in the world, with products ranging from coffee cake to women's underwear and from athletic gear to hot dogs. But that was to be the future. For the time being, Cummings began to acquire. In 1942, he acquired Sprague Warner Company, distributor of Richelieu canned goods, a well-known brand at that time. With this acquisition, he became the largest grocery distributor in the United States. In 1944, he bought Western Grocer Company and its subsidiary, Marshall Canning. In 1945, he added Reid, Murdoch Company and its famous Monarch brand. (Reid, Murdoch had been the first American company to import tea from India and China.) Next, Cummings acquired the company that later gave its name to the growing conglomerate. Here's how that happened.

The Sara Lee story begins in Decatur, Illinois, where a man named Charlie Lubin worked in the bakery business. He had become an apprentice baker at age

To get a feel for what people wanted to buy, Cummings liked to visit the stores that bought his products and serve customers himself.

14 and finally became a bakery assistant for "A & P" supermarkets in Chicago. With this experience, he and his brother-in-law decided in 1935 to go into business for themselves. They scraped together $1,500 and bought three small retail bakeries. For the next 14 years, Charlie Lubin baked and sold out of these three stores. Along the way, he felt that quality, premium-priced baked goods could be sold in supermarkets, which were just beginning to grow in America. In 1940, this was a wild idea. Experts said it wouldn't work. After all, the whole reason for supermarkets was low price!

Charlie Lubin thought otherwise and went ahead with the idea. First, he introduced cheesecake, then pecan all-butter cake, then pound cake. He used fresh milk, the finest butter, pure cream cheese, and fresh, whole eggs. Supermarket customers loved the quality of these products, and Charlie Lubin's business began to take off. He figured then that he needed a brand name to cover his entire line of good-tasting baked goods. His wife suggested Sara Lee, the name of their 8-year-old daughter. So, the name of the company became "The Kitchens of Sara Lee." (As an adult, Sara Lee even began to appear in the company's commercials.) Some time later, Nathan Cummings and Charlie Lubin got together. Sara Lee became part of Cummings's company, and Charlie stayed on to run the bakery division.

To broaden his holdings further, Cummings wanted to add a meat brand to his lineup. He had heard about the Bryan Packing Company that processed and sold meat products in Mississippi and went there to look at the business. Not only was this his first trip into the Deep South, it was also the first business trip for his daughter, Beatrice, whom he brought along so she could learn about business dealings. Cummings was charmed by southern hospitality and was also deeply impressed by a young man, John Bryan, who was managing the meat business for his family.

Cummings bought Bryan Packing in 1968, but John Bryan stayed on to run the operation. Not only did the company grow, but Cummings thought so much of Bryan that he persuaded the young man to come to

Sara Lee Lubin (top) slices a cake with her father, Charlie, at her side. Charlie, who began his career baking cakes one by one, inspects his mass-produced products (below).

Chicago and work with him. There they worked together, with Cummings testing and evaluating Bryan to see if he might be the person who could replace him and eventually head the company.

The partnership worked. Cummings taught Bryan about the business and passed along to him his street smarts and business savvy. Bryan, on the other hand, with a Harvard business degree and other advanced schooling, began to supply the missing ingredients of management that Nate Cummings, a man with no formal education, lacked.

In 1968, Cummings also bought Electrolux, a huge door-to-door business that sold vacuum cleaners, and then bought another famous name, Fuller Brush, which sold hair brushes and other household products. That same year, Cummings, age 72, decided to retire from active management of the business.

Under John Bryan, who became chief executive officer in 1975, the company continued the strategies of Cummings. They acquired Douwe Egberts, a Dutch company that produced coffee and tea and was a major brand in Europe. Some years later, and again following the Cummings plan, a major move was made into a completely different kind of business with the purchase of Hanes, a leading name in women's hosiery and lingerie.

Next, the company founded by Cummings bought Kiwi, an Australian business that was the world's biggest maker of shoe polish. Then they bought Dim, a French company that was the biggest producer of hosiery in Europe. They also bought Hillshire Farm, Jimmy Dean Meats, Coach Leatherware, and Champion Products, a fast-growing manufacturer of recreational athletic gear.

Two other acquisitions of major importance were L'eggs, one of the biggest names in hosiery, and Aris Isotoner, which had more than half of the glove market in the United States. As years passed, naming a consumer field of any kind in which the company did not have an interest became increasingly difficult.

With so many different products now being sold by the company, the name Consolidated Foods no longer fit: the word *Foods* did not work well with a business that also sold leather goods and women's hosiery. To pick a new name, the company did a large consumer research project. Somewhat to their surprise, they found that by far their most recognized name was . . . Sara Lee!

As they thought more about renaming the company, they realized that this name could cover just about any product category. And so, in 1985, the company became Sara Lee Corporation. The choice was a good one: Sara Lee was one of the best-known brand names in the world, and it was also a woman's name. After all, most of the company's products are both purchased and used by women.

For more than 30 years, Nathan Cummings had run his business in a highly personal way, calling on his instinct, intelligence, and ability to size up a situation

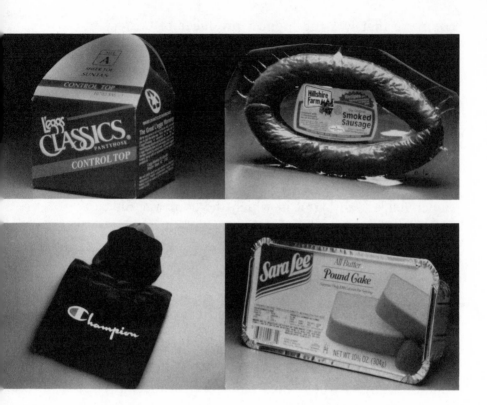

A few of the wide range of familiar products from the Sara Lee Corporation

quickly and make a decision. He left in his place a smart, well-educated, and strong young man to carry on. Often the person who starts and builds a business does not plan on who will run the company after the founder is gone. Many successful businessmen make this mistake, but Nathan Cummings didn't. When Cummings retired from active management, he remained a member of the board of directors and the executive committee. Thus, he participated in most of the major decisions. He also kept other ties in the business community. For example, he continued as a director of General Dynamics Corporation of St. Louis.

Early in his career and partly because of the influence of his daughter, Cummings learned to appreciate fine art, and he began to collect pieces from all over the world. His fame as a businessman grew and so did his art collection. He lined the walls of his apartment in New York City with the work of great artists of the past. And, as the years went, many visitors from around the world came to see his collection.

As the number of pieces in his collection grew, Cummings allowed some of them to be viewed in public museums, such as the National Gallery of Art in Washington, D.C., the Metropolitan Museum of Modern Art in New York City, and the Art Institute of Chicago. To the Metropolitan, he eventually made a gift of more than 600 pieces of pre-Colombian works, which may be seen in a gallery of the Michael C. Rockefeller wing.

Because Cummings was also deeply interested in medicine and science, he contributed to the Michael Reese Hospital, the Medical Center of Chicago, and the Nathan Cummings Basic Sciences Building at Mount Sinai Hospital in New York. The Cummings Life Science Center at the University of Chicago is one of 22 buildings around the world that he has endowed. He gave $5 million to the Memorial Sloan-Kettering

Cancer Center in New York, and at the time of his death was a trustee of Mount Sinai.

Cummings was also a life governor of the Jewish General Hospital of Montreal, an officer of the French Legion of Honor, and a *Commendatore* of the Order of Merit of Italy. He held honorary degrees from Catholic University in Washington, D.C., and the University of New Brunswick in Canada. He also received an honorary Doctor of Philosophy from Tel Aviv University in Israel.

Nathan Cummings gave his daughter, Beatrice, full credit for teaching him the value of public responsibility. She helped him see that successful people have an obligation to be good citizens. And she urged him to give a percentage of the company's annual income to various health, education, welfare, and arts organizations. Good citizenship, she told him, was good business. And he listened well.

Almost to the day he died at 88, Nathan Cummings was active and involved. He spoke by phone to John Bryan on a weekly basis and, at the time of his death, planned to attend the company's next board meeting. He was a man of huge energy and positive attitude. He had a powerful handshake, and when anyone asked him how he was, he would always say with enthusiasm, "I feel great!"

Although the owner of a very large business, Cummings was always willing to listen and ready to take advice. Among his many strengths were perseverance,

In the Nathan Cummings tradition, John Bryan continued both the practice of acquiring companies and contributing generously to society.

determination, and an unwillingness to accept defeat. Perhaps his finest quality was his optimism; even when something big had gone wrong, he would tell his young partner, John Bryan, "Don't be discouraged, there's always another deal."

Since his death, his company has created the Nathan Cummings Youth Ambassadors Program. In this exchange plan, each year ten children of Sara Lee employees in the United States live in the homes of families in other countries. Through this program, the company hopes to give children the opportunity to understand different cultures and different countries.

The program is open to all teenage children of Sara Lee employees. Youth for Understanding, a non-profit organization in Washington, D.C., administers the programs and makes the selections.

John Bryan said about Nathan Cummings after his death: "I think Nate Cummings illustrates the two qualities most important to be successful in business. The first of these traits is, without question, integrity. . . . If you're not as good as your word—if you do not deal honestly and fairly—you won't last long in the business world. . . . The second quality to be successful in business is perseverance. Nate Cummings stuck it out through bankruptcies, through the Depression of the 1930s, and against all odds. From a very modest beginning, he built a company that I and so many others are proud to work for. And we're proud of him because of his generosity to society."

Cummings's daughter, Beatrice, said of her father, "The principles that guided his life became my own personal principles. . . . [They are a] willingness to work hard for goals, excellence in performance, discipline in one's life and community service. . . . The concept of privilege and corresponding responsibility has been the model for his children and grandchildren and for his nieces and nephews as well. I hope that he is remembered as having made the world a little better for having walked this way."

Finally, we have the words of Nathan Cummings himself, whose favorite comment throughout his life was "If you want anything in this world, you have to work hard for it, and you have to make it your priority."

What Nathan Cummings, the son of poor immigrants, accomplished in business is truly remarkable. But what he accomplished, the legacy he left, his contributions to science, medicine, and to his community, is not merely remarkable . . . but is almost beyond belief!

In 1944, Bud Hillerich, age 78, commemorates the 60th anniversary of his Louisville Slugger by turning a baseball bat on the lathe.

6

Bud Hillerich:
The First Bat Man

*T*his story is about of the most famous name in baseball bats, the Louisville Slugger. It is also the story of the true genius of a very young man with no formal business training and, in fact, very little schooling. His name was John Andrew "Bud" Hillerich (pronounced Hill-rick), and the name of the company is Hillerich & Bradsby, a name that everywhere in the country means one thing: baseball bats.

The story goes back more than 130 years to the city of Louisville, Kentucky, where John Fred Hillerich owned a small wood-turning company. Louisville had several such companies. Wood-turning was a common business in those days, producing such things as newel posts for canopy beds, banisters for stairways, bowling balls and pins, and even beer faucets. The work was done mostly on lathes, and Hillerich made these products for carpenters, shop owners, and homeowners in the area. His plant was tiny, 20 by 30 feet, and he employed only a few workers. The little business was honest, well run, and it made products that people wanted and needed.

In 1880, at age 14, young Bud joined the company. In those days, a son often came into the family business, but the long-term impact of what Bud was going to do was far from anyone's mind. Bud had at least two qualities that made him different from other boys going to work to learn a trade. First, he was a good baseball player, and, second, he had an imagination and spirit of innovation. This spirit, well down the road, would lead to the marketing idea that today is connected with Michael Jordan and other star professionals: the endorsed sports product.

The big sport in the country at that time was baseball. And Bud Hillerich was a baseball player; not full-time, of course, because he had to work. But he was good enough to be a semi-pro, which meant he made a little money for his skill. He was a player who understood the art of hitting and had a deep appreciation for the wooden bats that produced hits. Being in the wood-turning business, he made his own bats. If something went wrong with a bat he was using, he would go back to the factory and fix it. Soon he was making bats for his teammates and, as the word got around, he began making them for other semi-pro players around Louisville.

At that time, Louisville had a professional team in the American Association called the Eclipse, and Bud Hillerich went to as many games as he could afford. Like thousands of young men of his day, he was a real fan. The Eclipse had an outfielder named Pete Browning, the team's leading hitter. For 13 years he was one of the best hitters in the entire league. One day when Bud was at the game, Browning broke his bat. After the game, Bud approached Browning and invited him back to the plant where Bud said he would make him a new bat. The two men spent the night working together, Bud gradually turning the wood into a bat, then handing it to Browning to see how it was shaping up. Finally, they got it just right, and the next day, Pete Browning got three hits!

Browning was a colorful character, and word got around about his new bat. He was a natural hitter and had a very personal relationship with his bats. He named each one, and when he felt it was "out of hits," he retired it and put it in a special place in his house. Ballplayers then were very superstitious (as many are today), and a bat became either a friend or an enemy. If a friend, the player treated it carefully and did not offend it in any way.

Bud Hillerich understood the feelings of ball players about their bats. One player might want a bat longer than normal, another might want a bat that had a narrow grip, still another looked for light weight. Bud was certain that almost every player wanted a special bat,

Pete Browning, nicknamed "The Gladiator," used custom-made Louisville Sluggers to achieve a .341 lifetime batting average. His career lasted until 1894, when he played for the Brooklyn (later the Los Angeles) Dodgers. He died in 1905.

varying somewhat from the norm. Yes, custom-made was the answer! He knew that this idea would have huge appeal to almost every hitter.

Bud also knew that ball players wanted some kind of edge when facing a pitcher. With this in mind, Bud gave a name to his bats, the Louisville Slugger, which not only set it apart from other bats on the market, but also gave it a special personality, an idea that today is called "image." So the Louisville Slugger became the brand name for an entire line of bats made by the Hillerich factory.

During this time, however, not all was going well for Bud. His father, J. Fred Hillerich, did not like the idea that his tiny factory, hardly large enough to handle the basic wood-turning business, would be making baseball bats. After all, the main business, the business that brought in the most money, had nothing to do with baseball. J. Fred had little money, and putting his limited capital into making bats was not part of his plan.

The main part of Fred's business and the part that he understood and loved was wood-turning—making traditional products that people needed. In the late 1880s, the biggest portion of his business and the one that showed the most promise for the future was making butter churns. And at exactly the time that son Bud was dreaming his baseball dream, father Fred got a contract to make 600 butter churns, a huge order, the biggest in the company's history!

Many people in those days made their own butter in wooden churns. The new model developed by J. Fred would churn butter in just six minutes. The large order meant that he needed money to buy wood and to purchase additional storage space. J. Fred borrowed the money, planning to use it to purchase more wood for the butter churns. Once he had filled the large order, he could then further expand the plant, pay back the bank loan, and keep a roof over the heads of his family.

So, J. Fred and his son were on opposite sides of a business problem. The father needed every available dime to put back into the business so that he could make and sell more butter churns. The son wanted to make baseball bats.

Long-bearded J. Fred Hillerich (second from left) and son, Bud (in doorway with bat), pose with employees of the world's first bat factory around 1887. Bud's bat rests on a butter churn, the company's main product. A stylish bed post, another important product, stands to his left.

Bud Hillerich, rapidly becoming a smart and talented marketer, knew from practical experience that he could make and sell only a limited number of bats for local ballplayers. If he wanted the bat business to grow, and if the idea of a brand name for bats was to catch on, he had to figure out how to sell bats beyond the limits of Louisville. He had to get into wider distribution in other states where semi-pro and professional baseball was played.

Making a few bats for a few players was not enough. He had to make lots of bats for lots of players, and this meant more wood, more production, more space, and better distribution methods. Under the circumstances, with his father strongly opposed to the idea and the business problems, huge for an inexperienced young man to face, it is amazing that Bud figured out how to bring the project together and make everything work.

What problems did he face? Many. He had to learn how to make bats faster. This he did by inventing a centering device on the lathe on which the bat was turned. Thus, other workers—not just Bud—could produce bats. Obviously, this accomplished the objective of increased production. Next, he conceived the idea of pre-cut wood (ash was best), four inches by four feet. He called these blocks of wood *billets*. They could be stored easily while waiting their turn on the lathe. Next, he invented an automatic sanding system that made the bat smooth and gave it a quality look. So, by 1888, Bud had solved one important problem—how to make customized bats faster.

But an even bigger problem existed. How could a bat be called custom-made if it was actually turned out in large numbers? And here Bud Hillerich came up with an idea that has not only survived all the way to today, but is probably the biggest idea in the history of sports equipment marketing! He decided to make a certain style of bat and call it the "Pete Browning" model or the "Arlie Latham" model. (Both men were baseball stars of the time.) The brand name "Louisville Slugger" set it apart from all other bats, and the style, or model, was that of a popular player. This is so accepted today that the idea may seem very simple, but at that time, the concept was new and different. The success of this idea through the years and what it has become in modern sports marketing make it extraordinary!

Bud took this unique idea a step further and actually used Pete Browning's signature on the bat. Thus, people knew that this was the personal model used by the leading hitter in the American Association. The idea took hold and was the key to the enormous success of the Hillerich & Bradsby Company. Through the years, baseball players have used the Babe Ruth model, the Ted Williams, the Mickey Mantle, the Hank Aaron, the Roger Maris, the Joe Morgan, the Reggie Jackson. The idea, of course, has gone far beyond baseball bats to hockey sticks, running shoes, to gloves, and to the biggest sports phenomenon of today—Michael Jordan's "Air Jordans."

In 1890, Bud's father, realizing that wider distribution was also the key to expanding his butter churn business, signed an agreement with the Simmons Hardware Company of St. Louis to handle sales outside the Louisville area. The Simmons company was in the business of distributing products made by other companies. Getting their products distributed to stores is a problem for many companies, and neither J. Fred Hillerich nor Bud had experience in distribution. But they were smart enough to see that they needed this type of help.

Each had different reasons for wanting wider distribution. Bud wanted to sell baseball bats, and his father wanted to sell more butter churns. Of course, the butter churn business would not be around forever, but neither J. Fred nor Bud had any idea of that in the 1890s.

Still, the biggest problem of all remained to be solved: in which direction would they turn? Somehow the father and the son made a series of basic decisions that would forever affect the future of the company. In 1897, they gave the company a new name—J. F. Hillerich & Son. They acquired more property in order to get more space. They made contracts with lumber companies to make sure they had a steady supply of the kind of wood they needed. And they divided the business into two distinct parts—making wood churns and other traditional products and producing baseball bats.

Bud Hillerich, as a junior partner, could now make decisions without having first to ask his father. He was able to concentrate on the baseball part of the business, and he went at the job with enthusiasm and the sound instincts that would always be important to its success.

In those days, the total number of baseball bats used by professional teams was probably no more than 3,000 a year. Bud was making just a few hundred. With his improved and faster production, he figured he could make about 3,000 for the pro players, which would give him a solid hold on that market. But he saw far beyond that rather limited opportunity to a much bigger one.

*Hall of Famer Nap Lajoie, a .338 lifetime hitter, became the
American League's first star in 1901 when he batted .422,
hit 14 homeruns, and drove in 125 runs.*

Bradsby took over the company's sales responsibilities
and was so good at it that in 1916 his name was added to
the business.

Bud Hillerich died in 1946, at age 80, on his way to
a baseball meeting in California. Ward, his elder son,
took over but died soon after in 1949. As a result, the
younger son, John A. Hillerich, Jr., became president.
He managed the company until 1969, when his son,
John A. Hillerich III, succeeded him.

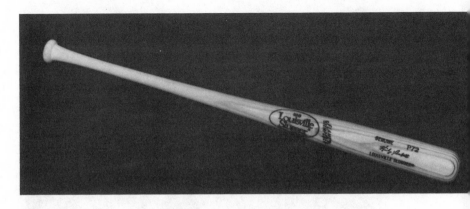

Personalized Louisville Slugger bats remain popular with baseball's top players—much as they were more than 100 years ago.

Today, Hillerich and Bradsby makes more than 1.5 million Louisville Slugger bats. Although the major leagues still require the players to use only wooden bats, most bats used today are aluminum, because they last longer and are less costly.

Bud Hillerich brought huge talent to the family business and built the company through incredible marketing creativity. Would "Air Jordans" exist today without Bud Hillerich? Probably, because if he had not thought of the endorsement idea, someone else would have. But the fact is that he did it first!

John Andrew "Bud" Hillerich. Skilled wood-turner. Ball player. Inventor. Smart business manager. Marketing innovator. Builder. A true pioneer who left an everlasting mark not only on baseball, but also on the entire world of sport.

Before he divided his wealth among family members, Sam Walton was called the richest man in the United States—a label that embarrassed him and one he didn't care to talk about.

7

Sam Walton:
Discounting to Riches

A lot has been written about Sam Walton having been America's richest man. Whether this is true or not, no one really knows. Sam Walton did make a lot of money in his lifetime, but that really isn't the point. What Sam Walton accomplished in that life is far more important.

Sam Walton was born in March 1918 on a farm near the Oklahoma town of Kingfisher. A younger brother, Bud, was born in 1921, and he was to play an important role in the retail empire Sam started and built years later. In his autobiography, Sam says he sold magazine subscriptions when he was about seven years old. The family, if not poor, was pretty close to it, and they all worked hard. By the time the Great Depression of the

1930s came along, Sam's family had left Oklahoma and were living in a small farm town in Missouri, where Sam went to school.

Sam played both football and basketball in high school, and both teams won state championships. Sam was quiet, didn't use swear words, and became an Eagle Scout. He milked the family cow, sold the milk, and did odd jobs to make money and help his family. He was president of the student body, and his classmates voted him the "most versatile boy." His ethic was work, work, work. He became known as a boy who didn't waste time.

In the fall of 1936, Sam started his freshman year at the University of Missouri. He worked his way through college, earning money from a paper route and serving as a lifeguard at the municipal swimming pool. He was also a captain in the ROTC (Reserve Officers Training Corps). He was president of his senior class and elected to an honorary society of men "devoted to their school." Years later, Sam said that when he graduated from college, he was very tired and had put in more hours and worked harder "than at any other time in his life."

Sam's college major was business, and although he was interested in insurance as a possible business career, he decided that retailing would be better for him. He was interviewed and hired by the J.C. Penney company and went to work in their Des Moines, Iowa, store at $75 a month. He plunged into this job, not dreaming where it would one day lead him. The company gave

Early in his retailing career, Sam Walton learned the value of motivating his employees.

Sam a copy of *The Penney Idea*, which was a written philosophy and operating manual. Sam smiled, thinking it a bit silly, but as he thought more about it, the concept became serious to him. Penney was a leader in modern retailing and a major innovator in dealing with customers and employees, whom the company called "associates." The whole idea was to put customer service ahead of profit. Everything Sam learned at the J. C. Penney store in Des Moines would help him later in life.

During World War II, Sam became a second lieutenant. In 1943, he married, and, in 1945, was discharged as a captain. A few weeks later, he went to
Newport, Arkansas, with his wife and 11-month-old
son. There he had a chance to buy the local Ben
Franklin Five-and-Dime store. The Ben Franklin system, like other chains of that time, allowed each of their
stores to be individually owned and operated, as long as
established guidelines were followed. This was Sam's
first experience in business for himself.

Not only did the store do well from the start, but
Sam also got into community affairs and later became
president of Newport's chamber of commerce. As head
of the chamber, he persuaded the president of a company that made metal tubes for Colgate toothpaste to put
their plant in Newport, which meant 650 new jobs for
the town.

As owner of the five-and-dime, Sam worked all the
time and soon paid back every nickel he had borrowed
to buy the store. A bit later, he brought his brother,
Bud, into the business as assistant manager. Years later,
Bud would become a very valuable asset to the Wal-
Mart company.

Sam loved retailing. It fascinated him, and he was
always looking for ways to increase business and make
things run better. At one point, he borrowed $1,800 to
buy an ice cream machine. That summer, he put the
machine out in front of the store and sold ice cream as
fast as the machine could turn it out! In the first full

year of the store's operation, it did $105,000 in sales, and just two years later, $175,000.

But in 1950, he ran into his first serious business problem. When he tried to renew the lease on the Newport store, he was shocked to discover that he did not have the option to renew. The people who owned the building decided that they wanted it for themselves. Now Sam had to find a new town in which to buy another store. He never forgot this tough lesson.

This time, he ended up in Bentonville, Arkansas, which eventually became the headquarters for Wal-Mart. Bentonville was a true southern town, a close community and hard to break into, but Sam threw himself into the job of making the store successful and becoming a part of the town. He studied the history of the town and spoke to many of its long-time residents.

In 1952, Sam bought another store, in Fayetteville, Arkansas. Shortly after, he and Bud bought a store together in Ruskin Heights, Missouri. With his stores and suppliers spread over many miles, Sam was spending much of his time simply driving from place to place, leaving little time for much else. He began to think about how he could operate many stores at once and at the same time cut down on his travel time. Then he hit upon an idea; why not fly from town to town instead? So, he bought a secondhand plane, learned to fly, and as the number of stores he owned increased, he flew constantly from place to place, saving many hours of time. He later said that without flying, Wal-Mart would never have happened. Over the years, he logged more than 10,000 hours of flying time and was said to be a natural pilot, if not a careful one.

Every day, though Sam spent time on hundreds of details and problems, he never lost sight of his long-term goal of owning more and more stores. And he never stopped thinking of new and better ideas to increase business. For example, when the hula hoop craze hit America, Sam tried to buy as many as he could from the original manufacturer. When he couldn't get the number he wanted, he set up a little plant to make his own. And he sold them as fast as he could turn them out!

Of the stores that Sam operated in the late 1950s, none was doing better than the one that he and Bud owned in Ruskin Heights, which had sales of $350,000 annually. The success of this store, located in a shopping mall, made Sam want to expand into more malls. But to do this required more money than he had, and he pulled away from the idea before it cost him too much.

By 1960, Sam was operating 15 stores—working 16 hours a day—and doing $1.4 million in sales. Although he couldn't be with his family very much, they did take camping trips together. Sam loved the outdoors and was an enthusiastic quail hunter. For the rest of his life, Sam managed to fit quail hunting into all his other activities and would often hunt in the early morning before going to his office.

Sam's wife, Helen, mostly raised the children, who,

when old enough, worked their own paper routes, as young Sam had many years earlier. They lived a simple life, and no one could tell that the family had more money than most. When they decided to build a new house in Bentonville, however, their architect was a student of the famous Frank Lloyd Wright, who built them a home wrapped around a brook. As time went by, the home became the center of many Wal-Mart employee parties.

By the early 1960s, Sam's ideas for the future were even bigger, and he cut back on his civic activities to

Always an enthusiastic salesman, Walton found that big profits could be made by selling merchandise at low prices.

devote even more time to the business. Never afraid of a new idea if he saw a competitor do something he felt his stores should be doing, he copied it. (And usually did it better!) When he heard about the new retailing idea called "discounting," he flew to New England to study it in the area where it had started. The idea was to put all kinds of merchandise in very large warehouse-like buildings, buy from suppliers at the lowest possible cost, and sell the products at prices lower than ever offered before. Some of the companies he visited were Mammoth Mart, Spartan's, and Zayre.

Sam went to Chicago to talk to the top management of the Ben Franklin system about building Ben Franklin discount stores in small towns. Changing the basic business strategy of Ben Franklin to discounting was something the top management of Ben Franklin would have to approve. And they would not. In fact, they turned him down. Sam decided that if he could not bring discounting into the Ben Franklin stores, he would create his own chain of stores. Then he would be free to manage them the way he wanted.

In late 1962, while flying from one town to another, Sam and one of his top advisors were talking about what to name the new stores. They discussed one name, then another. Finally, the other man wrote the name Wal-Mart on a piece of paper. It's short, he said, and it has part of the Walton name. And the word "mart" tells customers that it's a store. Sam did not react to the suggestion, and then the man did a shrewd thing: He pointed out that manufacturing and lighting signs for store names cost a lot of money. The name Wal-Mart, being short, would cost little to make into signs. Again, Sam said nothing, but in a few days the sign went up on a brand-new store in Rogers, Arkansas: Wal-Mart. In the first year, 1962, the sales volume was $1 million.

In 1964, Sam's company opened Wal-Mart stores in the towns of Springdale and Harrison, Arkansas, and although the opening day of the Harrison store was a disaster, the discounting idea was off and running. By 1966, Sam had 4 Wal-Marts and 18 Ben Franklins. One man who knew Sam well called him a "modern day version of Vince Lombardi," the pro football coaching legend of the Green Bay Packers. This may or may not have been an accurate comparison, just as the comparison between Sam and General George Patton of World War II fame. But Patton supposedly had said something like this during the war: "A good plan violently executed *now* is better than a perfect plan next week." And that sounded like Sam Walton!

It is probably more true that Sam Walton was neither like Lombardi nor Patton. He was the first to say that his success was not entirely due to his own work. He was very good at recruiting good people, getting top men and women to work for him. And his wife, Helen, helped a lot, advising him on many decisions. One person wrote that his greatest characteristic was efficiency. Another wrote that it was frugality, that he was very careful with a dollar and hated waste. Another said that

Sam developed tremendous loyalty among his people. When a store manager was doing an extra good job, Sam often rewarded him right on the spot.

When an architect designed a new headquarters building, Sam threw the whole plan away, cutting back the office space and vastly increasing the warehouse space. "The warehouse space makes us money," he said. Sam paid well, and expected much. One of his sayings, which he repeated often, was "Do it; try it; fix it." He tried to know what was going on in his stores. And if he didn't, he'd get in his plane and find out. Often, in his plane, he would fly to as many as seven or eight different towns a day, checking each store.

The kind of expansion and constant building that Sam did required a lot of money, and although his business was doing well, it was not bringing in the vast amount of money needed to build all of the new stores he wanted. Sam was already millions of dollars in debt so, in 1969, he decided to go public. That is, he sold stock in Wal-Mart to the public. When the stock finally came out, it sold fast. (An investment of just $1,650 in 1970 was worth more than $3 million in 1990.)

Everything was moving very fast. Sam opened 14 new stores in 1971 and the total sales increased by 77 percent—an amazing figure! By 1974, he had 78 Wal-Marts and was still not satisfied. Some people called him a slave driver. An employee could come to work at 6:30 in the morning, and still be working at midnight.

A meeting could start at 7 o'clock in the evening and last three or four hours.

Sam's principles included hard work, honesty, fair play, courage, faith in God, kindness, discipline, and great stubbornness against the odds. He was never a man to stand still just because things were going well. He changed direction often, seeming sometimes, as his people said, "to be riding north and south at the same time."

Sam wanted no frills, no expenses beyond those that were absolutely necessary. At the company's board of directors' meetings, he offered potato chips for snacking, but board members who wanted a soft drink had to buy it with their own money. When his people came to company sales meetings once or twice a year, they would often sleep as many as eight to a motel room to save the company money. He did not allow his employees to accept gifts from suppliers, and he forbade men and women of the company from dating each other.

Sam's driving habits were well known around the company. Once he bumped into one of his own trucks—a truck driven by a driver who had won a company award for careful and safe driving. Another time, he left his hunting truck parked on the main street of Bentonville, forgot it, and walked home. His executives thought someone had kidnapped him! Sam laughed when reminded of it; he could forget his truck, but he never forgot anything that was directly connected to the business.

As he reached the age of 56, Sam turned the business over to a man he had been grooming for several years. At this point, the company had 104 stores and 6,000 employees; just a year later, it had 175 stores and 7,500 employees. Even though he had replaced himself as head of Wal-Mart, he still came to the office every day and continued to fly his airplane around the eight states in which the company was doing business.

Then, in an incident that shook the entire company, Sam dismissed the man he had chosen to replace him and became chief executive again. Some people had been unhappy with the way the man ran the company, and Sam realized that he really didn't want to retire after all. Neither Sam nor the man he dismissed gave detailed explanations about exactly what happened, however. After this, Sam continued to look for top people to help the company grow. By 1979, he had 229 stores in 10 states with 17,500 employees.

Wal-Mart had become a giant, but it was still run in the same way by the same man, who simply refused to slow down. At about this time, always looking for ways to widen the company's pool of talented people, he added a woman to his board of directors—Hillary Rodham Clinton. She was no ordinary woman; she was a member of a leading Arkansas law firm and the wife of Bill Clinton, governor of Arkansas. In 1993, she became first lady when her husband entered the White House as the 42nd president of the United States.

In 1979, Sam's top two executives came to him to try

Sam greets a few of his more than 300,000 Wal-Mart associates.

to persuade him to install computers throughout the company. They argued a lot about it. Sam had two objections. First, wouldn't installing computers in the business side of the company cost a great deal of money, possibly as much as $500 million? Second, what could computers do for them that they weren't getting done now? The two men finally convinced Sam to spend the money, and computers helped Wal-Mart tremendously.

Sam freely admitted the value of the computers, but he also argued that people, not machines, were the company's most valuable asset. Still, once Sam made his decision, he gave computers his full support and never once attempted to be negative about this kind of modernization.

As the 1970s ended, Sam continued to build more

new stores, and Wal-Mart moved into even more states. But competition was getting tougher. This in itself did not bother Sam, but it concerned him that some of his people may have been getting complacent. He knew how important it was to stay ahead of competitors who were trying to take business away from them.

However, now another and far more serious problem arose. Sam had always worked hard, probably harder than any of his people, and had seemed to relish the long hours and the never-ending problems. But now he felt tired all the time and often could not find the energy that he needed to do the kind of job he wanted to do. Finally, he went to the doctor and learned he had a disease called hairy cell leukemia, a cancer that the medical profession knew little about.

Sam consulted with several doctors and clinics and, though refusing surgery, agreed to use, almost on a test basis, a new drug called interferon. After continuous treatment for many months, his leukemia went into remission, and Sam went ahead with his projects. He felt, at least for the moment, that he had beaten the disease, but always in the back of his mind was the knowledge that his mother had died of cancer. He thought that perhaps his mother had somehow passed along the likelihood of the same problem to him. But he was so pleased with the success of the interferon treatments that he gave $200,000 for additional research.

Now Sam's main project became the establishment of his own wholesale clubs, huge stores with vast amounts of merchandise under one roof. If a person paid a small annual fee, she or he could shop for almost all the household needs at huge savings. The name he gave these stores was Sam's Club.

In addition to expanding his discount stores, Sam throughout the 1980s was busy buying more banks (he had bought his first bank some years earlier), a newspaper, a shoe manufacturing company, and a jewelry company. He also set up a satellite system so he could talk to all his employees at the same time, without having to travel all over his widespread system.

Wal-Mart sales were now in the billions of dollars, and just about anyone who had worked for the company for any significant period of time could retire with enough money to live comfortably. Sam had established profit-sharing early on, and this gave each employee the opportunity to accumulate fairly large sums of money. For example, one worker—not an executive—left the company with more than $200,000 in her profit-sharing trust fund. Because Sam gave his people many benefits, labor unions were unable to unionize the employees and gave up trying.

Sam was rich, yes, but magazines could no longer name him as the richest person in America, for he had split his money among his family. Earlier, when Sam was first listed by *Forbes* as the 19th richest person in the United States, he wrote the editor of the magazine, saying "I could kick your butt for ever running that list!" In 1985, he was listed as the richest person in the U.S., with Texas businessman H. Ross Perot ranked in second place.

Because Sam had so much money and because the fact was well known, he was constantly approached by hundreds of organizations asking him for money. In order to control this, he set up the Walton Foundation to make decisions on all requests for charity. Because Sam was so interested in education, the foundation gave millions to colleges in several states. Television personality Robin Leach said Sam should be president of the United States and run the country as he ran Wal-Mart.

During the 1980s, Sam was given the Libertas Award for being a champion of free enterprise. In 1986, he won the Gold Medal from the National Retail Association. And in March 1992, President George Bush gave Sam his country's highest civilian award, the Presidential Medal of Freedom.

Going into the 1990s, while Sam was still working hard at beating archrival K-Mart, he was also taking aim at the giant—Sears. He was convinced that he could catch and pass Sears as the country's largest retailer. As fate would have it, the end of 1992 saw Sam's company indeed top Sears, but Sam Walton was not there to see this happen. In 1989, he was diagnosed as having cancer of the bone. Although he continued working as hard as he could, his energy was limited, and he was increasingly frail. On April 5, 1992, Sam Walton died.

Books and articles about this amazing man usually emphasize how much money he made. But his main

At the end of 1992, the company Walton founded 30 years earlier became America's largest retailer, with sales surpassing $50 billion.

accomplishment was the building of the most successful retail store system in history, giving employment to thousands of people. He did this with one simple idea—*the customer comes first.* Sam Walton was an honest man who worked very hard, loved his family, revered his country, and relentlessly pursued a dream. He made the dream come true, and that is what he should be given credit for. Because, when it comes down to it, that's what success is.

Rose Totino mixed her kitchen skills and Italian heritage to create a multi-million dollar frozen foods business.

8

Rose Totino:
The Pizza Lady from Minneapolis

Not far from downtown Minneapolis, Minnesota, is a section of the city sometimes called "Nordeast." For many years, first and second generation Russians, Poles, Ukrainians, and Italians lived there. These people chose to "live Nordeast" because they felt comfortable with people of similar ethnic backgrounds, generally from countries of Eastern and Southern Europe. Strong ties held them together, and still do. Most large cities of the northern United States have such areas, and it was here that Rose Cruciani was born in 1915, fourth in a family of seven children. Her parents, born in Italy, moved first to Pennsylvania, then to Minneapolis.

Like most of the people in this book, Rose Cruciani experienced the Great Depression, when millions of people were out of work and money was scarce. Dropping out of high school at 16, she did house work for a few dollars a week to help her family get by. In those days, young women often stopped school and began to work so that the young men in the family could either continue school or learn a trade in order to become the main wage earners later. This was a carry-over from the European traditions of their mothers and fathers.

Rose met a young man, Jim Totino, and after going together for a while, they married. Jim had taken up the baking trade, and Rose, learning from her mother, became skillful at making a kind of Italian pie, using sausage, cheese, and various types of sauces. Today, you know this as pizza. Of course, by now millions of people have eaten pizza, but in Rose's time, only a small number of Italian households knew about it. At first, Rose prepared pizza to serve to people who dropped into their home for neighborhood and church meetings. After tasting it, friends suggested that she and Jim open a little restaurant and serve pizza as a main meal.

Rose and Jim talked about this idea. They figured that $1,500 would get them started. They went to a bank, and Rose, with a good sense of what might impress a banker, brought along one of her freshly baked pizza pies. The banker was so taken with the taste that they got their loan!

Rose and Jim figured that if they could sell 25 pizzas a week, they could pay the rent on the restaurant. If

A courtship picture of Rose, 18, and Jim Totino.

business increased, they could slowly pay off their bank loan and maybe keep a little for themselves. At the end of each business day—often as long as 18 hours—they would be so tired that they would take the money they had earned and stuff it into a brown paper bag. The next day, Rose would take the bag with her and pay the people they owed.

As the days went by, even after paying their immediate bills, money was left over. Rose, with her basic business instinct, knew they had something. After just three weeks, the new business was doing so well that Rose persuaded Jim to quit his bakery job (he had been working at both the restaurant and the bakery) and come into their little business full time. Jim would bake the crusts; Rose would prepare the sauces and toppings. Within a few years, the restaurant was booming, and they had actually saved $50,000!

When an offer came along to buy the business, they considered selling, but they were still young and knew they'd be bored. Soon after, they ran into problems that every young business faces, and it was obvious that changes had to be made. They were turning out as many handmade pizzas as they possibly could, and this limited the growth of their business. In addition, some customers who came a long way to the restaurant told them that they should put their pizzas into supermarkets where they would be more convenient to buy.

Rose and Jim decided to do this, but they could not handle the large number of pies needed to supply supermarket demands. Their extremely slow production now worked against them, and with increasingly higher costs from suppliers for the ingredients that went into their pizzas, they began to lose money. In fact, they were losing money so fast that bankruptcy was near! They were desperate.

At a baker's meeting in Dallas, Jim learned a new way to produce crusts faster. However, they needed money for machinery, and this time the bank turned their request for a loan down. In real trouble, they went to a U.S. government agency, the Small Business

Administration, and asked for $50,000. But working with the government meant many delays and lots of paperwork, and in the meantime, they struggled day to day to keep their business going. They worked hard, yet they were losing money and going deeper into debt.

One day, while Rose was driving to work, she heard

It's lunchtime! In the Totino company kitchen, Rose shows her delight at having made another tasty pizza.

an announcer on her car radio talking about how God loved each and every human being. The words moved Rose beyond anything she'd ever listened to. When she got to the office in the pizza store, a man from the Small Business Administration was there to tell her that the loan was approved. She later gave $1,000 to the radio station to show her gratitude.

The new method of preparing pizzas for supermarkets worked, and within several months, the business was back on track and making a profit. To meet the demand, Rose and Jim put on a second shift of workers and also began to build a second plant. Business was so good that an eager buyer offered them $1 million dollars for it. But they said "No." Some years after that, Totino's Frozen Pizza became the biggest selling pizza in the United States.

Then, when Jim Totino's health began to fail and the business needed a new multi-million dollar plant to keep up with demand, Rose and her top managers knew that it was time to sell. So, in 1971, with Jim in obvious decline, Rose decided to sell the business. Any number of companies were willing to buy, but one of them, Pillsbury, was a Minneapolis company, and she felt they would be best. Rose finally decided to sell to Pillsbury, in 1975, not only because they were a local business (which was important to her) but also because "Pillsbury believed in research and development." Pillsbury paid more than $20 million for the business, and Rose, age 60, went to work for the new owners at $100,000 a year.

Totino's pizzas provide steady sales and profits for Grand Metropolitan PLC, the British conglomerate that bought Pillsbury in 1989.

And so she became one of the top female executives in the world of business.

The head of Pillsbury, a man named Bill Spoor, with whom Rose developed a deep friendship, promised her she'd have a secretary for life, and that she could stay with the company as long as she wished. Her contract was for five years. During the early 1990s, she was still with Pillsbury and no contract was needed.

The Pillsbury headquarters are in downtown Minneapolis, but Rose had her office in a huge building across the Mississippi River in the company's Technology Headquarters. Strangely enough, it was only a few blocks from the Totino's restaurant in her beloved Nordeast where she was raised and spent most of her life.

Rose's job at Pillsbury was to make sure that the quality of the pizza products remained high and to develop new products. But she did even more. In her late seventies, Rose Totino was still the best salesperson for the line. She traveled all over the country, conducting seminars, meeting brokers and salespeople, and winning new customers. She also appeared on TV talk shows and did interviews with newspaper writers. She called her work "the most fun thing I've ever done!"

As a human being, Rose Totino had many remarkable qualities. Warm and personal, she spoke well and had a delightful sense of humor. In her office, she would make a visitor feel comfortable. As a business person with no formal training, her instincts were sound, and her method of arriving at decisions worked very well. She never claimed to be a marketing expert, so when she realized many years ago that marketing pizza would become critically important, she hired the people she needed. And after hiring them, she listened to them and did mostly what they recommended.

When Rose still owned the company, her employees gave her full credit for hiring them and letting them do their jobs. One long-time employee said, "Everybody who worked there thought it was a marvelous place to be. The Totinos got the best out of their people because they trusted them." Rose believed that "if you tell people what their objective is, and that you depend on them, usually they will do a good job."

In the early days, when the business was growing so

fast it often was close to being out of control, Rose's good instincts told her that she had to take certain steps to get things pointed in the right direction. The business needed growth, and opening up new cities (called "markets") meant plowing more and more money into it. At the same time, the future of her company meant continuous investment in what is called research and development—the constant improvement of quality, the search for better ideas, the drive to stay ahead of the competition. Partly by luck, but mostly because she was such a sound thinker, Rose made the right decisions.

In June 1994, more than 40 years after she had decided to start her own business, Rose Totino died of cancer. She was 79 years old. As those who knew her will attest, Rose was much more than an executive. Rose Totino was an absolute giant of truth and compassion and love. A successful business person, by all means. But even more important, a successful business person who was also a magnificent human being.

John H. Johnson, founder and chairman of multi-million dollar Johnson Publishing Company, succeeded in the business world in spite of the racism that he faced.

9

John Johnson:
"Don't Get Mad, Get Smart"

*T*his chapter is about the most successful black businessman in North America. He is far richer than thousands of white business people whose names are much better known. He is worth many millions of dollars (only he knows exactly how much), and he still heads the company he founded in November 1942. Although his business is privately held (which means the amount of business it does is not public information), many estimate that the annual volume is more than $300 million. This incredible man is John H. Johnson, who runs Johnson Publishing Company, which publishes three magazines—*Ebony*, a general interest magazine; *Jet*, a weekly news magazine; and *Em*, a monthly men's magazine. He also owns radio stations, a TV production company, a travel service, and the world's largest traveling fashion show.

Part of this country's romantic history is that many famous people—presidents, painters, philosophers, poets—were born in log cabins and rose beyond their beginnings to wealth and fame and power. John Johnson fits this history. He was born in a shack with a tin roof in the small town of Arkansas City, Arkansas, in 1918. His home was cold in winter, hot in summer, and not very comfortable anytime.

Johnson today does not complain about being poor. "We always had enough to eat," he says. His real father was killed in a sawmill accident, and his stepfather delivered groceries. The family had very little, but as Johnson says in his autobiography, *Succeeding Against the Odds*, life wasn't completely bad.

Johnson learned how to work when he was very young, long before his teens, and never had time for sports. Life for most black families in the South during the Great Depression was grim. More than half the blacks in southern states were unemployed, so many of them left for the North. A large number settled in Chicago, which was thought of as a kind of "promised land." According to the stories, Chicago had jobs, education, and freedom. Against the advice of her husband, Johnson's mother, Gertrude, moved herself and her son, John, to that huge city, mostly so he could continue school. They arrived in 1933, a low time in a dreadful series of Depression years.

During high school, the bad times forced John and his mother to go on welfare, then called "relief." While necessary for survival, relief was degrading and humiliating. Discussing welfare later in life, Johnson said, "The problem, I think, is the purpose of welfare and the organization of the welfare system. The goal must always be to *get off* welfare." Johnson's mother fought her way off as fast as she possibly could.

With his Deep-South drawl, homemade clothing, and bow legs, John was made fun of by his city-wise classmates. But he worked hard, concentrated on civics and journalism, and eventually became editor of the school paper and president of his senior class. He had two friends who went on to great fame in show business: the popular singer Nat "King" Cole, and John Sanford, who became comedian Redd Foxx. John Johnson was the only student speaker at the class of 1936 commencement of DuSable High School, and he titled his speech "Builders of a New World."

The main speaker at John's graduation was a black named Harry Pace, who was president of a successful insurance company—Supreme Liberty Life Insurance Company. When Pace finished speaking, John went to talk to him. Pace asked him what he was going to do next, and Johnson said he wanted to go to college, but his scholarship at the University of Chicago was for only $200, and he needed more than that. Pace told Johnson to come see him "in the fall." That September, John started as an office helper at Supreme and was assigned desk space right outside Pace's door. He was paid $25 a month and went to the University of Chicago part time.

Gradually, the work at Supreme became so exciting that John gave up his idea of studying law and went to work full time. (Years later, he said that all young people, especially blacks, must have a college degree for any chance at success, but at that time, "my real school from 1936 to 1941 was the university of Supreme Life.")

Some time after starting at the very bottom, Johnson was given a chance to work on the company's monthly newsletter. Later, he became assistant editor and, in 1939, the editor. In his autobiography, he calls this job "a strategic post for an ambitious young man." It gave him a chance to learn from successful men. He learned how to size up situations and make decisions, and he discovered that his future was in his own hands. Letting situations run him was bad, but *controlling* situations would further his own interests. He also learned the importance of letting his helpers do their own jobs (called "delegating"). But more importantly, he found that a good manager must constantly check, double-check and even triple-check, never taking anything for granted.

As editor of the company paper and as a student of journalism, John recognized an opportunity—no magazines were being written just for blacks. He thought that a monthly digest of facts of interest to, and about,

142

blacks, would make a good magazine. It would be, he thought, something like *Reader's Digest*, pulling together from various sources articles that would appeal to black men and women.

But John's idea, wonderful as it may have been, needed money to make it happen. He needed about $500 to get started. But he didn't have that amount and didn't have a clue as to how to get it. No one loaned money to blacks, and even whites had trouble borrowing in those times. One white banker, however, gave him a tip—if Johnson could get some *collateral*, the bank would lend him the $500.

Collateral, Johnson learned, was something of value that the bank could take if he did not pay off the loan. He then asked his mother if she'd let him offer their furniture as collateral. At first, she refused, but he kept talking (persistence being one of his many talents) and finally his mother let him use the furniture to get his money.

What a business person does with money once he or she gets it is as important as getting it in the first place. John could have used his $500 in many ways, but what he did was buy postage to mail letters to the names of black people on the Supreme Liberty mailing list, people whom he figured would be interested in such a magazine. His letter to the people on this list asked if they would be interested in buying such a publication. In the letter he included another smart idea. If the people liked the magazine concept, they should

Even as a young man Johnson recognized that education was the key to overcoming poverty.

send in $2.00 for a subscription. This brought in a whopping $6,000 in cash! The money allowed him to start up the magazine, which he called *Negro Digest*. This was the beginning of what was to become a giant business empire, but it began with an office so small that its first employee had to sit out in the hall.

Now John had his money, his list of subscribers, and an office, but he still had to get out a magazine. He wrote hundreds of letters to other magazines and newspapers for the right to reprint certain articles that had already been published. As if this problem wasn't difficult enough, he had to persuade a printer to give him credit so the magazine could actually go on the printing press. Somehow, he overcame these problems and out came the first issue of *Negro Digest*, 7 1/2 inches by 5 inches, in two colors. It carried articles by many famous writers of the day, some white, some black. *Negro Digest* was actually under way, and it attracted a fair amount of publicity, always a good break for a new business enterprise.

But John had to deal with other problems. The first issue, though attractive and full of good writing, had to be available on newsstands in Chicago so customers could pick it up and buy it. To get on newsstands, he had to have a distributor, and the distributor he called laughed at him, saying no one was interested in such a magazine.

What did Johnson do? He asked several of his friends to go around to various newsstands and ask for the new magazine. This worked very well and newsstand dealers began asking the distributor to give them the magazine so they could sell it. Now came the next problem: with the magazine in place on the newsstands, it had to sell. To help solve this, John sent his friends around to buy copies of *Negro Digest*. This gave the impression that the magazine was popular and selling fast.

Johnson had to buy back these copies from his friends, and the money he used to buy them back came from the amount he was going to use to pay the printer for doing the first issue. But the ruse worked. The distributor asked for 1,000 more copies and the newsstands started advertisng them to blacks. Soon he had enough money to pay the printer.

Within eight months, *Negro Digest* had a circulation of 50,000, most of the readers being educated blacks who wanted to read stories of interest to them, not to whites.

By far Johnson's biggest problem, day-by-day and hour-by-hour, was lack of enough money to operate the business properly. Of course, this is usually a problem for anyone starting up a company, but for a black man fighting racism as well as economics it was even more difficult. The magazine *was* a modest success, but it was not producing enough money for Johnson to stay ahead and to keep building. He did not have the option of simply going to a bank and getting the dollars just by asking. He constantly had to apply every ounce of his natural creativity.

One good example of his inventiveness was writing a letter to subscribers offering them lifetime subscriptions for $100 each, which brought in enough cash to keep him going for a while longer. But there were always bills to pay, and he was constantly facing the problem of which bills had to be paid immediately and which could be put off a bit longer.

In November 1945, Johnson started *Ebony* (all his businesses were begun in the month of November), which was to be a black version of *Life* magazine. *Ebony* continues today, five decades after its first issue was published. Johnson faced and solved a huge early problem for *Ebony*, and what he did is a wonderful example of his determination to succeed.

During World War II, the War Production Board, a government agency, told Johnson he could no longer obtain the amount of quality paper he was using to print the magazine. By this time, he was selling hundreds of thousands of copies. This was not discrimination (white businessmen also were limited), but rather

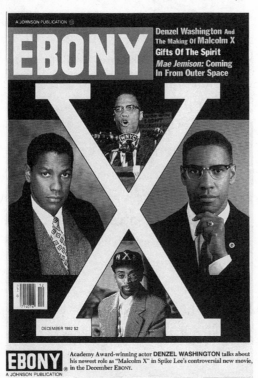

Johnson's Ebony *magazine cover featuring the popular movie* Malcolm X

a part of the government's policy of carefully watching certain materials necessary to the war effort.

Johnson, facing the destruction of his business, hired the best lawyer he could find, a fellow who happened to be a white man. Together, they worked out a plan that was brilliant in its directness and simplicity. Rather than go to Washington with his white attorney to argue the case, he would go, instead, as a poor black man trying to hang on to his little business, without any of the power of the white businessmen using their shrewd and skillful lawyers to plead their case. The strategy worked perfectly. Johnson's was the only one of 30 businesses that got the government to reconsider its position. He received the quality paper in the amount he needed, and he continued in business.

After the war, Johnson began to expand his publishing business. In 1951, he started *Jet*, a pocket-sized celebrity magazine something like *People* is today. In 1969, he changed the name of *Negro Digest*, his first publication, to *Black World*. From 1969 through 1975, *Black World* was full of controversy and good writing. Many described the magazine as "militant." But as the years went by, it began to lose money, and Johnson ceased its publication. Some blacks criticized him for this decision, but he answered them by saying, "I'm in business to make a profit." And that was that.

He continued to expand his enterprises with the purchase of a radio station in Chicago (WGRT, now WJPC) and acquired another in Louisville.

In 1992, Carol Moseley Braun became the first black woman elected to the United States Senate. John Johnson, one of Braun's Illinois constituents, put her on the cover of his Jet *magazine.*

Johnson also began a line of cosmetics, called "Fashion Fair," and ran cosmetic ads in his publications. Within a few years, Fashion Fair became a highly profitable business, with sales of more than $430 million a year.

The cosmetics business is different from others in that it requires trained sales people to call on department stores. At that time, however, few blacks were trained in sales. Tackling this problem head on, Johnson went out with one of his own people, and together they called on major stores like Marshall Fields and Bonwit Teller. They learned on the job.

Today, the line is sold through more than 1,500 stores worldwide.

Next Johnson began planning a TV production company to produce black programs. And he still had time to start *Ebony Jr.* for preteens. To help provide positive images for young blacks, he searched for likely black role models.

Johnson is probably the most powerful and influential black businessman in America. He owns his own skyscraper in Chicago, a condominium in Chicago, and a home in Palm Springs, California. On top of a mountain, it's just up the road from Bob Hope's house. He has been, and still is, an advisor to U.S. presidents, and is on a first-name basis with the Kennedys, the Nixons, Carters, Reagans, and Fords. He knows hundreds of people in the world of entertainment and music. He has succeeded in a world dominated by whites and has done this with a combination of hard work, mental toughness, a willingness to try and try and try again, and the courage to take a chance.

John Johnson is a powerful spokesman for black causes, black education, and the idea of blacks returning to their neighborhoods to start businesses. Although he calls his success a miracle, in reality the words "smart" and "hard work" fit better. He takes nothing for granted and lives every day as if he could lose the entire business tomorrow. In this philosophy, he stays ahead of problems and is always looking for new ideas to keep his company vital. He is a tough taskmaster and a stern father figure to every Johnson employee.

Johnson says, "There is no such thing as security. Nothing is guaranteed. What you've got to do is have small goals, not large ones. Small goals are easier to attain, and you can get discouraged if you pick large ones. For years, I tried to get someone to join me in a venture to build a skyscraper in Chicago. Nobody wanted to go in with me, so I finally did it alone, building a smaller one.

"Sure," Johnson added, "I want blacks to try for joint ventures, or get loans from banks, but when that fails, and it often does, then they must be creative about their own financing. If a black wants to be his own boss, then he's got to go out there and make waves. He's got to start something, build something, create something." Johnson knows that *Fortune* magazine has called him a tough boss. "Yes, I know that, but tough does not mean I go around bullying people. Tough means I hold people accountable," he said

John H. Johnson, born in a tin-roofed shack in a tiny southern town, is one of the most influential men in the United States. But he still doesn't believe that everything will work out all right. So, in his seventies, and not believing in retirement, he still works hard.

The word "success." The words "hard work." The words "overcoming obstacles." These words probably fit John Johnson more than anyone else whose story appears in this book.

Afterword

Writing a book like this without help is difficult. Many people helped me, and I want to thank them.

I'd like to share with you how this book came to be. In the fall of 1991, I was reading the Minneapolis Star Tribune. One of its stories was about a well-known business person. The story was not favorable, and that surprised me because I knew the person. The person I knew did not seem anything like the person the paper was writing about. I thought that the reporter was trying hard to write about only negative things.

The more I read, the more clearly I realized that the reporter was making the business person look bad simply because this person was successful—a successful business person running a successful company. I thought that was unfair and poor journalism. So I wrote a long letter to the newspaper. The letter was about how badly our press often treats successful people.

To my surprise, the newspaper printed my letter, and it appeared on December 15, 1991. My letter received considerable reaction, including many letters and some phone calls. In fact, I got 189 letters from men and women who said it was about time someone wrote a letter like mine. I got three letters from people who disagreed with me, and one letter that was so confusing I wasn't sure what its writer was trying to say.

One letter was from a publisher who thought the point of

my letter might make a good book for young people. I agreed to choose some well-known people who had started successful companies and write a chapter about each person. We both felt that a book telling of such people would be interesting to youth and that youth could learn from it. Because I didn't personally know any of these people and because most of the people are deceased, I wrote their companies and asked for information that would help me to write the book.

So, many people did help me with this book. I'd like to thank the following: Cheryl Davis of the Walt Disney Company; Jon Firestone of BBDO Advertising Agency; E. Ronald Culp of Sara Lee Corporation; the public relations department of Hillerich & Bradsby; the promotion department of Johnson Publishing Company; Leon Gorman of L.L. Bean, Inc.; and Mark Abels of Northwest Airlines. Each sent me helpful information.

I also did two personal interviews. One was with Rose Totino herself, and I thank this most fascinating and gracious woman for the time she gave me. To help write the chapter about Northwest Airlines, I spent some time with retired 747 pilot Vince Doyle, who has a treasury of material about that company.

And finally, two more "thank-you's" are in order. This book would not have happened if the Minneapolis Star Tribune *had not printed my letter in December 1991. And a final thank you to Mark Lerner of The Oliver Press, who saw my letter and thought it was worth a book for you to read.*

—Bob Pile
Minneapolis, 1993

Bibliography

Drucker, Peter. *Innovation and Entrepreneurship*. New York: Harper & Row, 1985.

Fox, Stephen. *The Mirror Makers: A History of American Advertising and Its Creators*. New York: Morrow, 1984.

Fritz, Roger. *Nobody Gets Rich Working for Somebody Else*. New York: Dodd, Mead & Co., 1987.

Greene, Richard, and Katherine. *The Man Behind the Magic: The Story of Walt Disney*. New York: Viking Press, 1991.

Johnson, John H. *Succeeding Against the Odds*. New York: Warner Books, 1989.

Mills, Stephen. *More Than Meets the Sky*. Seattle: Superior Publishing Co., 1972.

Perot, H. Ross. *United We Stand*. Westport, CT: Hyperion Press, 1992.

Pine, Carol, and Susan Mundale. *Self-Made: The Stories of Twelve Minnesota Entrepreneurs*. Minneapolis: Dorn Books, 1982.

Ruble, Kenneth D. *Flight To The Top*. Minneapolis: K.D. Ruble, 1986.

Trimble, Vance. *Sam Walton: The Inside Story of America's Richest Man*. New York: Dutton, 1990.

Walton, Sam. *Made In America*. New York: Doubleday, 1992.

Index

Ford Tri-motor, 21
Foxx, Redd, 141
Freeport, ME, 29, 30, 39, 40,
    42
Fuller Brush, 88
Funicello, Annette, 62

General Electric, 69, 73
General Mills, 71
General Motors, 69, 71
Gorman, Leon, 38-41, 43
Grand Metropolitan PLC, 135
Great Depression, 35, 55, 56,
    94, 111-112, 129-130, 140

Hanes, 88
Harvard Classics, 68
Hillerich, Bud: as baseball play-
    er, 98; bats made by, 96, 99-
    100, 102-104, 105, 106; death
    of, 108; early years of, 97, 98-
    101; and Louisville Slugger,
    96, 100, 103-104, 107; pro-
    duction methods of, 103,
    105, 106; qualities of, 98,
    105, 109; relationship of,
    with father, 100-103, 105
Hillerich, John Fred, 97, 98,
    100-102, 104-105
Hillerich, John, Jr., 108
Hillerich, John, III, 108
Hillerich & Bradsby, 97, 104
Hillshire Farm, 89
Holman, Charles "Speed," 20,
    24

interferon, 124
interlocking ownership, 25-26
Iwwerks, Ubbe, 47, 49, 52, 53,
    54

Jazz Singer, The, 52
Jet, 139, 148, 149
J.F. Hillerich & Son, 105, 106
Jimmy Dean Meats, 89

Johnson, John H.: as business-
    man, 138, 139, 143-144, 148,
    149; and cosmetic business,
    149-150; early years of, 140-
    141; as editor, 142; financial
    problems of, 141, 143-144,
    145, 146; magazines of, 144-
    146, 147, 148; qualities of,
    142, 146, 150, 151; wealth of,
    139, 150
Johnson Publishing Company,
    138, 139
Jolson, Al, 52
Jordon, Michael, 98, 104, 106,
    109

Kenny, C.D., 82-83
Kitchens of Sara Lee, The 86
Kiwi, 88
K-Mart, 126

Lajoie, Napoleon, 106, 108
L'eggs, 89
leisure market for sports equip-
    ment, 106, 107
Lever Brothers, 71
Lewis, Fulton, Jr., 26
Life, 147
Lindbergh, Charles A., 18, 21
Little Mermaid, The, 65
L.L Bean, Inc., 29; catalog of
    29, 33, 35, 37, 39, 40; cus-
    tomers of, 42-43; and envi-
    ronmental issues, 43; estab-
    lishment of, 35; growth of,
    35-36; under Leon Gorman,
    39-43; problems of, 37-38,
    39; sales of, 29, 35, 37, 40;
    written guarantee of, 32, 33,
    34, 43
Lockheed 10-A Electra, 25
Lousville, KY, 97, 98
Louisville Slugger, 10, 96, 97,
    100, 103-104, 107, 109
Lubin, Charlie, 84, 85-86, 87

137; early years of, 129-130; employee treatment of, 136; qualities of, 131, 133-134, 136, 137; as owner of pizza company, 132, 134, 136-137; restaurants of, 130-132, 135

Totino's Frozen Pizza, 134, 135

True-Life Adventure films, 60

Twenty Thousand Leagues under the Sea, 60

Twin Cities, 15, 16, 18, 19, 21

United War Work Campaign, 69

Universal Pictures, 51

U.S. Army Air Corps, 25

U.S. Rubber Company, 34

U.S. Steel, 71

Wagner, Honus, 106, 107

Wal-Mart, 114, 115, 117, 118-119, 120, 121, 122, 123, 124

Walt Disney Productions, 50

Walton, Bud, 111, 114

Walton, Helen, 116, 119

Walton, Sam: awards of, 126; death of, 126; early years of, 111-112; employee treatment of, 121, 125; and establishment of Sam's Club, 124-125; health of, 124, 126; involvement of, in community affairs, 114, 126; as owner of five-and-dime stores, 114-115, 116, 118, 119; as owner of Wal-Mart, 118, 121; as pilot, 115-116, 120, 122; qualities of, 112, 115, 117, 119, 120, 121, 127; wealth of, 110, 111, 125-126

WED (Walt E. Disney), 60

Western Grocer Company, 84

Williams, Ted, 107

wood-turning, 96-98, 101

World War I, 14, 46, 68

Wright brothers, 12

Wright, Orville, 20

Photo Credits

ABOUT THE AUTHOR

ROBERT PILE retired in 1980 as senior vice-president of one of the country's largest advertising agencies. He spent 38 years in the advertising industry. His clients included Tonka Toys, Procter and Gamble, Pillsbury, National Car Rental, Dairy Queen, and La Choy. He has written and published two novels, as well as a book on European travel. Pile has also written numerous articles about business, travel, and golf for several newspapers and magazines. In addition, he is the author of the forthcoming book, *Women Business Leaders*. Pile has taught "Principles of Advertising" at the University of St. Thomas, St. Paul, and he currently serves on the board of directors of two companies. During World War II, he was a pilot in the Army Air Corps. Pile has six children and lives in Minneapolis.